Decisions

From The Dais

"Five Pillars" of
School Board Governance in A Post-
Pandemic World

Keith C. Wolaridge

Decisions From the Dais
Copyright © Keith C. Wolaridge
December 2023

Published by Pearson Self Publishers
www.pearsonselfpublishers.com

Printed in the United States of America

Meet Keith Wolaridge

Keith C. Wolaridge is a retired, award-winning, former bank executive and veteran school board trustee. Since 2009, he served as an elected school board trustee for Panama Buena Vista Union School District in Central California, where he has seen the district grow in the number of schools, budget, and student population. In addition, Keith is an Associate Professor of business at his local community college and owns an online learning academy specializing in coaching emerging non-profit school boards, and a school's classified staff. Known as a business and community leader, Keith is a husband of over twenty years and father to four beautiful daughters. He's an avid golfer and loves to read. His life's mission is to make a positive impact by providing solid instruction, instantaneous inspiration, and imparting life-changing insights to all he comes into contact with.

Get to know Keith better! Visit him at:
www.keithcwolaridge.net ... and ... www.fivepillars.me.

To future students of the
United States of America.
This book is dedicated to them.

Table of Contents

Preface

In a remote African village named Ujima, nestled in the heart of the Savannah, the concept of collective governance was deeply ingrained in the community's values. One sunny morning, a young boy named Kofi was born to loving parents, Lulu and Tendai. The entire village rejoiced at the news of the new arrival, for they believed that each child was a gift to the entire community.

As Kofi grew, it became apparent that he was a spirited and curious child, always eager to explore the world around him. The village elders, who had seen countless children grow and thrive, took a keen interest in Kofi's development.

They knew that it was not just the responsibility of his parents to raise him but the collective duty of the entire village. Whenever Kofi ventured out to play by the river, the village women watched over him as they fetched water, ensuring his safety. The men would teach him the ways of farming and animal husbandry, imparting wisdom about the land.

As he grew older, the elders would gather under the Baobab tree, the village's sacred meeting place, to discuss Kofi's progress and well-being. They shared stories with him of their own experiences and offered guidance on how to navigate life's challenges.

When it was time for Kofi to attend school, the village came together to build a small, thatched-roofed classroom. The children of Ujima learned side by side with the older children helping the younger ones, just as the entire village had helped raise Kofi.

Years passed, and Kofi grew into a wise and passionate young man. He respected his parents' teachings but also valued the wisdom of his village. He had learned that governance wasn't just about laws and leaders, but about a shared responsibility to support and nurture each other.

As Kofi stood at the threshold of adulthood, the village celebrated not only his accomplishments but also the strength of their governance system. They knew that it was the interconnectedness and shared values of Ujima that had molded Kofi into the remarkable individual he had become.

In Ujima, they believed their children were not only the family's future but the entire community's future. Through their collective governance, they fostered a sense of unity, wisdom, and love that would continue to guide generations to come, ensuring a harmonious and prosperous future for their village.

As school board members, it is our duty and charge to provide the best possible education for the Kofis in our communities. My name is Keith Wolaridge, and I have had the honor of being a school board member in my community for over 15 years. I have witnessed a lot and have been fortunate to serve on county and state-level educational committees and boards. I am not a perfect school trustee, nor is this book for everyone.

This is not an admonishment toward perfection, but merely my feeble intention to provide a guide for some, and a reminder for others, in regard to this massive responsibility. With any text inside this book, feel free to eat the meat and discard the bones.

There are ideas presented here that you may disagree with but, while you may disagree with my head, I ask you to listen to my heart. The purpose of this book isn't for complete agreement, but to encourage trustees to think about and bring whatever best practices back to your school boards for the betterment of the children we are elected to serve.

Chapter 1

The Call to Serve.
Understanding and Knowing Your "Why"

Who Are We?

So, you want to be a school board member? Congratulations on taking this wonderful opportunity to change young people's lives and improve our nation! Why do we have boards of education? Local government is the most crucial part of democracy in the United States. It's the foundation that has kept our country together through hundreds of years of ups and downs.

Authors Henry Brickwell and Regina Paul (1988) say in their text, *Time for Curriculum* that we use citizen control for "cities, counties, states, regions and the nation. We use it for sewers, police, roads, firefighting, rivers, libraries, airplanes, prisons, forests, the military, and every other government function." Giving control of our schools to people whose communities have chosen to run school districts and county offices of education makes sense.

School board members are the most common type of elected public official in the United States. Every day people. We are parents, neighbors, and community leaders from various backgrounds and professions. We vary in generations, from Baby

Boomers to Millennials. And many school board members are either current or former educators.

According to a study conducted by the National School Boards Association (NSBA), the nation's school boards reflect a better gender balance than either the United States Congress or the state legislatures in 2017. Only 19.6% of seats in the US Congress and 24.9% of positions in state legislatures were filled by women in 2017, while 50% of the nation's school board members were female.

The number of females holding school board positions has steadily increased from 39.9% in NSBA's 1992 survey to 44% in its 2010 survey. Board members continue to reflect a mature segment of the population, with a median age of 59 among those completing the 2018 survey—not a surprising result since nearly 70% were over 50 when this question was asked in 2010. (p. 3)

Although school boards are becoming more diverse, they don't reflect how quickly the K–12 student population is changing. The US Department of Education predicts that 48% of the 50.7 million students entering prekindergarten through grade 12 in 2017 will be white, 16% will be Black, 27% will be Hispanic, and less than 1% will be Asian/Pacific Islander, American Indian, or Alaska Native.

Nearly 3% will say they are more than one race. The majority of board members in the 2018 survey were white (78%), then African American/Black (10%), Hispanic or Latino (3%), and American Indian or Alaska Native (1%). (p. 4)

While not a prerequisite to serving, almost three-fourths of board members have at least a bachelor's degree, far exceeding the 29.5% of American adults over age 25 who hold at least a B.A. In large districts, 85% of board members have at least a B.A., and more than half report that they have earned an advanced degree of some kind.

Individual board members reflect the broad spectrum of political philosophies found across the general, American public, and among the 80% of 2018 respondents who choose to respond to this question, are almost evenly split among Progressives (23%). Those leaning Progressive (21%); Leaning Conservative (17%); and Conservative (19%). In 2010, the categories were labeled differently, with (20.3%) identifying as Liberal, (49.3%) as Moderate, and (30.3%) as Conservative (p. 9).

Role of a School Board Member

The primary role of a school board member is to set policies that govern the operation of schools in their districts. These policies should be designed to meet the educational needs of students and should reflect the values and expectations of the community. School board members work collaboratively to establish policies that ensure the safety and well-being of students, create effective instructional programs, and support the development of skilled and dedicated teachers.

School board members also serve as liaisons between the community and the school district. They attend public meetings, listen to concerns from parents, students, and community members, and communicate important information about the district to the public.

One of the main roles of a member is to work to build relationships with stakeholders, including parents, teachers, business leaders, and local government officials.

It has been my experience that school boards engage in:

- Recruit, hire, and evaluate the superintendent
- Approve budgets
- Set spending priorities
- Approve textbooks and other materials for the curriculum
- Set the annual school schedule and decide when schools will open and close.
- Work closely with school and district leaders on school schedules, supplies, safety, discipline, classroom resources, facilities, and other issues.

A good school board sets the vision for the students in a community and helps them get a world-class education that will prepare them for life after high school. Wider tasks include setting high academic standards, supporting teachers and staff, ensuring transparency and accountability, creating a safe and positive school culture, and pushing for policies that help every student succeed. Often there are disagreements on how to accomplish these tasks, but school boards try to reach a consensus, settle differences, find a middle ground, and, most importantly, find solutions.

Jim Burgett (2013), in his book, *"The Art of School Boarding: What Every School Board Member Needs to Know,"* summed it up perfectly: "Simply put, school governance is simply corporate governance in a school setting, with the fundamental goals of being accountable, fair, and transparent." (p.61)

The role of school board leadership is critical to ensuring the education system's success. Effective school board leadership can help create a shared vision for student success, establish policies and procedures that support student learning, and develop partnerships with stakeholders that foster positive relationships and trust.

The article, *"Effective School Board Leadership: A Synthesis of Literature"* by Catherine A. Lugg and James J. Gallagher (2007), examines the characteristics of effective school board leadership, including governance, communication, and collaboration. They state that governance is a critical aspect of effective school board leadership, and without it, chaos occurs. School boards are responsible for setting policies and making decisions that impact educational opportunities and outcomes for the next generation.

Effective governance involves developing clear policies aligned with the school district's mission and goals, ensuring compliance with legal and regulatory requirements, and effectively providing oversight to implement policies and procedures. Your role as part of this governance team involves setting clear expectations and goals for student learning and achievement. School boards must establish measurable goals that are aligned with the needs and priorities of the community and regularly monitor progress toward those goals.

The superintendent, district administrators, and staff are accountable for achieving the goals and objectives set by the school board. In our zeal to be influential board members, there is a fine line and balance between accountability and being overbearing. This is crucial to remember. While many see you as their boss, in reality, a trustee has only one employee: the superintendent.

An effective trustee understands their power and works with the superintendent to enforce and establish joint accountability standards. When establishing effective governance in school board leadership, it is crucial to ensure that district administrators and staff are accountable for achieving the goals and objectives set by the school board, but how one goes about that is where the art lies.

The following are some tips for establishing accountability systems without appearing overbearing. The critical point to remember is that if there is adequate support and acknowledgment of success, you will tend to be more successful. It is important to provide support to district leaders and staff. This means providing adequate resources to help them understand their roles and responsibilities and giving them the tools they need to be successful.

Communication is another critical aspect of effective school board leadership. Effective communication involves building relationships with stakeholders, including educators, families, and community members, and engaging in a two-way dialogue that promotes transparency and collaboration. Effective school board leaders should be able to communicate clearly and effectively using a variety of channels, including meetings, newsletters, social media, and other forms of media.

One of the key and vital pillars to effective school board leadership is that school board leaders should engage in ongoing, professional development that promotes the development of essential communication skills. School board leaders should be able to address the needs and concerns of stakeholders and work collaboratively to find solutions that promote student success. When done correctly, effective communication builds trust and credibility with stakeholders, which is essential for creating a positive learning culture.

Collaboration is also a critical aspect of effective school board leadership. Effective school board leaders should collaborate with school administrators, teachers, parents, and community members to develop a shared vision for student success. The hard work of collaboration involves seeking diverse perspectives, engaging in respectful dialogue, and building consensus around key issues.

This collaboration includes developing partnerships with stakeholders that promote student success. This can include partnerships with businesses, community organizations, and other educational institutions. Effective partnerships should be grounded in shared goals and objectives and involve a commitment to the success of all students.

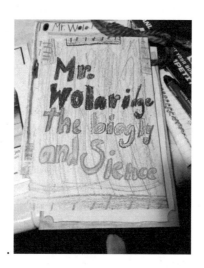

A handwritten card from a student expressing thanks for me coming to her classroom

Also, let's not forget to celebrate successes! It's important to celebrate successes when they occur. This helps to reinforce appreciation shown for their hard work as the board works with cabinet and district employees working toward the established goals and objectives.

Know Your Why

Like myself, many people decide to become school trustees

because they either have children in the district or a passion for education. Amanda, a school board member from my neighboring district, said she felt it was her responsibility to serve her community, and that serving on the school board was a tangible reason to do this.

I know of one trustee in Northern California who is known for her unwavering dedication to improving children's lives. She had a heart for the underprivileged and wanted to ensure they had access to quality education.

I have a friend who was bullied in school, so he ran because he didn't want any other child to experience what he did. Then there was my dear and abiding friend, Lisa, who was dedicated to bridging the achievement gap. She implemented a mentorship program, pairing successful professionals from the community with disadvantaged students and providing guidance and inspiration.

A Voice

American entrepreneur, Comer Contrell said, "The greatest inspiration is often born of desperation." (Quoteland.com: *Comer Contrell*). Many trustees expressed both political and personal frustration by running for their local school board. Two friends, Geri Rivera and Leigh Ann Cook, both ran because their children needed an advocate. Their children had special educational needs for which they felt the school could do a bit more.

In Geri's case, she was a stay-at-home mom with four very different kids with very different needs, from a high-achieving student to adopted children with mental health issues. She believed that she was a valuable asset and the voice of parents from whom the district was not hearing nor listening at the time, in a predominately Hispanic community.

Before being elected, she stated, "I saw things. Parents and staff would talk to me, ask me questions, and ask for help with my input, but I wondered why they were going to me and not the principal for the district. Then, I realized nobody felt heard or seen, so I decided I would bridge the gap between the lofty ideals of the administration and the real world of parents and employees."

Another trustee, Leigh Ann Cook, always wanted to serve in her community. Her son was diagnosed with ADHD and the school system missed his diagnosis in the first grade. It wasn't until he was older and retested that he was properly diagnosed. As a field representative for her county supervisor, she believed that running for school board was the next logical step in her professional progression to be a voice for those parents who didn't know how to use their voice or were lost navigating the special education department in school districts.

In his classic book, *Start With Why*, my favorite author and thought leader, Simon Sinek (2008), says it all starts with "clarity." You have to know *why* you do what you do. People don't buy what you do; they buy *why you do it*. So, it follows that if you don't know *why* you do what you do, how would anyone else?

Simon Sinek's "Know Your Why" is a powerful concept that resonates with millions of people worldwide. It's based on the idea that '*understanding the purpose behind our actions and decisions*' is the key to achieving success and fulfillment in life.

Suppose the leader of an organization can't clearly articulate why they serve, let alone why the organization exists beyond its products or services. How does he expect the employees to know why they should come to work? The same holds for school board members. Why do you want to do this work? What is your motivation?

At the heart of Sinek's message is that people and organizations should focus on their "why" the reason they exist and the purpose they serve—rather than just their "what" the products they sell and the services they provide. According to Sinek, when we understand our "why," we can better inspire ourselves and others, make more informed decisions and ultimately achieve greater success!

Sinek's ideas are rooted in the concept of the Golden Circle, a model he developed to illustrate the relationship between the "why," "how," and "what" of an organization or individual. The Golden Circle consists of three concentric circles, with the "why" at the center, the "how" in the middle, and the "what" on the outer edge. Sinek argues that most people and organizations operate from the outside in, focusing on the "what" and "how" without ever truly understanding their "why." However, those who can start with their "why" and work outwardly are more likely to achieve lasting success and inspire others.

One of the critical insights from Sinek's work is that our "why" is not about making money or achieving fame. Instead, it's about the impact we want to have on the world and, in this case, education and the legacy we want to leave behind. When school board members are clear about their "why," we can better align our actions and decisions with our values and beliefs, leading to greater fulfillment, impact, satisfaction, and success for the students and community served.

My current colleague, Brian Easter, states that he wanted to serve on the board and govern from a parent's perspective. That is why this service is of personal value and, being an educator himself, he wants to ensure a positive learning environment and outcomes without petty politics or agendas interfering with the work. In addition, Trustee Easter is an alumnus of our district and loves paying forward the opportunities afforded him while he was a student.

My cousin, De'shawn Woolridge, also a Northern California school board trustee, said that he didn't see anyone on the school board who looked like him, so as a schoolteacher and doctoral candidate, Mr. Woolridge raised his hand and ran. He was the youngest school board member elected. He felt his generation, 18–30, was left out of the conversation and he would bring a more hip and progressive voice to the district.

Public education is at a crossroads. My mentor and good friend, Bill Farris, recalls that he first ran for the board in 1983. He was a young businessman with children in elementary school and was aware of some community displeasure with the superintendent. His parents had taught him that we have a personal responsibility as citizens to serve and affect change as best we can.

Believing he could contribute; he ran for one of the three open seats and came in fourth. Approximately a year later, he was appointed to fill a vacancy created by a sitting member's resignation. Bill quickly realized that state and federal legislative restrictions significantly restricted the board's authority, which is why he discovered and redefined 'his why.' Now Bill has two supporting strategies:

1. The key purpose is to strengthen public educational opportunities for the children of our community.
2. Building a strong, effective governance team for advocacy and influence at the state and federal levels for local control, decision-making, and authority, which is crucial for school

boards.

Culture Wars

It would be naive of me to think that many of the candidates running for school board office have altruistic motives. When this occurs, it's because the trustee doesn't understand school governance and procedures. The seats on the school board are, in principle, non-partisan, but this is becoming less and less common across the country. Many run with a political agenda or have other reasons for holding the position. For many years, school boards have been launching pads for political ambition. I'm sure this happens all over the country.

For instance, some candidates run on the platform of firing the superintendent or the head football coach. Then the candidate gets elected and figures out they have only one vote, so they may not get to fire anyone! Or they do get enough votes and are now seen as firing the district operations leader without cause because no evaluation was ever done of the superintendent or opportunity for improvement.

In a 2023 article by Politico, it is mentioned that conservative states are already carrying out sharp restrictions on classroom lessons, LGBTQ students, and library books. Two former school board members founded the conservative and well-organized grassroots organization, Moms of Liberty. Members learn how to attract media attention, screen potential candidates, analyze educational policies, and get ready to run for office.

The Republican Party is trying to use school boards and critical race theory to mobilize their voters. The conversation has turned toward race, specifically fears that school boards are introducing critical race theory to the curriculum. Some conservative activists and politicians are using these worries to drive school board recalls and rally their voters in statewide elections. (Niergburh, 2021) This is not to infer that the Democratic Party has no political agenda. Liberal parents are ready to fight back against the right's heightened focus on school board elections.

Over the past few years, hundreds of progressive activist organizations and political action committees have created or reoriented themselves. *Red, White, and Blue* is another national, liberal organization that began endorsing candidates, distributing campaign signs, and training parents to speak out in favor of diversity programs, transgender accommodation, and gun control.

Two Florida mothers founded the *Florida Freedom to Read Project* to fight book bans, while two, New York mothers founded *Defense of Democracy* because they were concerned about what they perceived as Christian nationalists targeting school boards. (Kingkade, 2023)

One of the highlights as a trustee is reading to students.

There is a litany of reasons why someone would want to become a school board member. The person must search within themselves to discover their motive or aspiration for wanting to serve. School boards do not need zealots. School boards do not need ideologues. School boards need women and men who possess wisdom. Wisdom is the bridge between knowledge and understanding, enabling us to make informed choices and navigate the complexities of our world with grace and insight. This key virtue separates the great school board member from 'the average.'

Making a difference and serving on the school board is challenging and it's essential to carefully consider the commitments and responsibilities involved before deciding to serve." I believe my colleague, Cheri Olgin's, *purpose and why* factors were succinct when she stated, "I wanted to make a difference for the students and be a voice for the voiceless."

The following story highlights the power and importance of trying to make a difference:

There once was a man taking a morning walk at the beach. He saw that along with the morning tide came hundreds of starfish and when the tide receded, they were left behind. And with the morning sun's rays, they would die. The tide was fresh and the starfish were alive. The man took a few steps, picked one up, and threw it into the water. He did that repeatedly. Behind him was another person who couldn't understand what this man was doing. He caught up with him and asked, "What are you doing? There are hundreds of starfish. How many can you help? What difference does it make?" This man did not reply, took two more steps, picked up another one, threw it into the water, and said, "It makes a difference to this one!"

What difference are we making? Big or small, it does not matter. If everyone made a small difference, we'd end up with a big difference, wouldn't we? I'd like to know if there are statistics that show how future trustees came to their idea of serving. It may be something in the news, a church conversation, or frustration at the school site. I'm sure this is what sets the wheels in motion. In my case, I wasn't thinking about it until pumping gas, Ken approached me on a scorching August day.

My Story

Ken, a community member, was at the fuel pump beside me and after the ubiquitous "How are you?" he asked me if I had any kids in the district. I answered yes. Four.

He mentioned that there was an upcoming retirement on the board, and would I be interested in replacing him? While I enjoy national and local politics, I initially thought I was too busy, underqualified, or didn't possess the political money and moxie to serve. So, I said no. But Ken was persistent. He provided a few reasons as to why I should at least apply and talk with the superintendent.

After returning home, I went to the district's website and looked at the current trustees who had been elected, but I didn't see any people of color on the board, and this was another reason I didn't give it another thought. But I did have four children in the district and if I could "look out after my investment" I should at least apply. I went through the process, and the rest is history.

Serving on your local school board will allow you to shape the future of education in your local area and advocate for the needs of students, teachers, and families. In my case, one compelling reason to run for school board was the opportunity to promote equity and inclusion in education. As a member, you can create policies and programs that promote diversity, equity, and inclusion in schools, and work to eliminate disparities in educational outcomes. School boards have a critical role in ensuring that all students have access to a high-quality education, regardless of their background, income level, and other factors.

It has been a thrill serving. My engagement in ensuring students receive a well-rounded education that prepares them for success in college, careers, and beyond feels wonderful. I have been able to give back to my community and positively impact the lives of others. I love education and having a small role in improving education in my city, I believe in creating a better future for students and families and building a stronger, more vibrant community.

Do you have an agenda? Since beginning your service, you might also have analyzed your actions, contributions, and behavior. If you were in a position to change the world, how would you plan to do this? If you campaigned to replace the football coach or fire and replace the superintendent, be the watchdog for every penny spent. Or would it be to take care of your teacher, friends, and allies? So, what is it? Futures are at stake.

If a school board member or any leader can't articulate why they seek public office beyond the standard pat answers, consider your motivation to serve. Be honest with yourself. Is it to serve or climb the political ladder?

Take the time to answer these questions honestly. Here are my three ways:

1. A Passion for Education

I have a passion for education. Education is the license to compete in our society. While it won't guarantee success, it allows one to enter the game. My role as a school board member is to ensure the next generation has a better educational experience than the previous generation. A school board member's primary role is education. I believe that a great school board member loves education.

Members of school boards often say they want to improve kids' lives, give them a better future, or leave a lasting impression. Some will mention global competition or the need to respond to future trends. School board members should remind themselves frequently as to why they joined the board. Effective, focused, and committed leadership can be the difference between tepid results and terrific outcomes.

2. A Passion for Service

Part of the US Air Force's slogan is "Service Before Self." A school board member or any public servant puts others before themselves. The sacrifices of time, talent, and money demonstrate this.

Service is a gift that is often overlooked. Service isn't always noticed, but putting others before yourself is a beautiful trait in this role, even if it's becoming rare.

When I think about service, my father comes to mind. I can't remember a time when he wasn't waking up early in the morning to coach city and church league basketball. He was always on the go, always moving. Last to sit, first to stand. Serving was his oxygen. For the church, he enjoyed parking lot detail early in the morning, in the driving rain and the hundred-degree heat. Service was his middle name! In his book, *The Measure of a Man,* Martin Luther King (1988) wrote:

"The Breath of Life" is the dimension of life in which we are concerned with others. An individual has not started living until he can rise above the narrow confines of these individualistic concerns to the broader concerns of all humanity." (King 1959, p. 171)

King wanted us to understand service. It's one of those endearing qualities of a decent person. In a field where self-promotion and idolization are the norms, self-sacrifice should be celebrated. People who disagree with the false thinking of self-promotion should be respected and praised. As a member of the school board, it is hard but essential and necessary to put the needs of children ahead of those of adults.

3. Passion for Opportunity

We are taught in the African American community and culture that no one can take our education from us. I refer back to my parents who would say this to me time and time again. Black people have instilled this core value into our children across two and three generations. Houses, cars, and money come and go, but your education will always remain. I have the honor and privilege of teaching in prison where I see firsthand what can happen as a result of limited educational opportunities. As a school board member, your job is to create an environment where every child has the opportunity to learn. Granted, some will not take advantage of it, but we will continue to encourage that young person. But consider one student, perhaps on the verge or the fence, and placing the right program and teacher in his life could make all the difference. I believe we must remove hurdles even if just one may have the opportunity to reach the American dream.

Possessing a strong "why" provides direction and purpose. It helps members understand what they are working toward and why it's important. Your "why" can motivate you to keep going, even when things get tough

The Pandemic

The pandemic was the toughest time in my tenure as a trustee. Unfortunately, many school board members were personally accused of, and criticized for, not taking sufficient precautions to prevent the spread of COVID-19, such as by failing to implement mask mandates and adequate social distancing measures. Some school boards were accused of making decisions about school operations and policies without adequately consulting teachers, parents, and other stakeholders. I am sad to report that, whether for or against the safety protocols, each side brought out the worst in our society.

Amanda Frank, a local trustee in my community, conveyed to me that amid COVID, she wanted to quit. "I know I'm a pretty good trustee," she said, "and making good and thoughtful decisions. But dang, Keith, I came home and cried after how we were treated at some of those meetings. It was an awful time."

I remember one school board meeting where the board room was full of stakeholders polarized on this issue. There was a lot of anger in the room, resulting from both personal and internal frustration. After each member of the public had their opportunity to share how they felt the board should vote, I recall sitting quietly, listening, and reflecting.

As each board member responded to the public's concerns, I remember saying, "I feel like Solomon who has to decide what to do with this baby."

For those who need a refresher, in 1st Kings 3:16-28 of the Old Testament, we see a story of a dispute between two women claiming to be the child's mother. King Solomon is asked to decide who the actual mother is, and he proposes a plan to divide the baby in half with a sword and give each woman half of the child. One woman agrees to this plan, but the other woman begs the king to give the child to the other woman, saying that the child should be alive with the other woman rather than be killed.

Impressed by the second woman's selfless love, Solomon declares her to be the true mother and gives her the child. This biblical account is often cited as an example of Solomon's wisdom and fairness as a judge—and also his craftiness in exposing evil.

During this school board meeting, I didn't have a whole lot of time to make difficult decisions and discern what was right and fair. Solomon was faced with a difficult decision, but he made a wise and just ruling by considering the feelings and well-being of the child involved. For this trustee, using this story of Solomon taught me about the power and importance of fairness and wisdom in decision-making and the value of making difficult choices.

A school board member must constantly reiterate and truly mean that they are there for the children first and adults second. It's one thing to say, "I'm for kids," but actions in and out of the boardroom convey a different message. With a kid-first mindset, it was easier to understand the board's values and goals clearly, examine my beliefs, evaluate options, and choose the best path for all stakeholders.

A strong "why" is essential for leading and participating as a school board trustee. In this role, you will need a well-of knowledge to draw from that provides guidance and serves as a beacon that guides your actions and decisions. When the job gets tough, and it will, understanding and possessing a clear sense of your "why" will make you more likely to persevere through challenges and setbacks because you have a deeper understanding of the meaning and significance of this important work.

A strong "why" helps trustees make better decisions. When school board members clearly understand their values and goals, it's easier to evaluate options and choose the best path with your "why." This is when having a solid lodestar in school board governance comes into play.

During the pandemic, I took time to read to students over Zoom

Reflective Questions - Chapter 1

1. How do school board members balance the responsibility of setting policies and approving budgets with the diverse needs and expectations of the community they serve?

2. How can school boards ensure that their composition reflects the demographic diversity of the K–12 student population, especially considering the disparities mentioned in the text?

3. According to Simon Sinek's concept of "Know Your Why," how does understanding school board members' motivation and purpose contribute to effective governance, communication, and collaboration within the education system?

Chapter 2

Responsibilities and Ethics of School Board Service. Respect the Role!

Know Your Limitations

One who is eager to serve with unique ideas is an excellent candidate for school boards. But, knowing your limitations is vital if you are thinking of becoming a school board member. Unfortunately, many people miss it.

A problem arises when these ideas stymie and become destructive. There are guardrails for school board members. When they are not followed in your district, devastation and chaos are on the horizon.

The seminal book on school board management by Davis Campbell and Michael Fullan, *The Governance Core (2019)*, provides clear and overarching guidance. In a nutshell, school board governance comes down to five overarching principles:

1. Establish strategic directions and related outcomes
2. Providing ongoing policy direction and approval
3. Stewardship and support for the district's work
4. Oversight and accountability
5. Community leadership.

In his book, *10 Questions Every School Board Should Ask,* Ken Odom (2014) states:

"When we give responsibility to a group, that group necessarily seeks authority to exercise its responsibility. Unchecked, the result is a power grab. I believe that this is happening in education today because school board members have not adequately addressed the responsibility that their elected authority implies. Our unwillingness to accept responsibility for our actions fuels conflicts between and among powerful interest groups. It rests with us to check the power grab before it does irreparable damage." (p 31)

School board trustees are responsible for overseeing the management and administration of public schools. While their role is essential, several limitations and challenges can make it difficult to fulfill their responsibilities effectively. One limitation of school board trustees is that they are often limited in their decision-making power. Addressing these limitations may require changes in laws and regulations, additional resources and support for trustees, plus greater collaboration and communication among stakeholders in the education system. A clear understanding of roles and responsibilities is vital to school board governance. Without it, the district becomes a mess, as more time is spent fighting and putting out fires between members.

Trustees must work within the confines of laws and regulations set by higher authorities, such as state and national governments, which can restrict their ability to make changes or implement new policies. This can make it difficult for school board trustees to address pressing issues or respond to emerging needs within their district. For many school districts, their state legislatures make up the laws and rules and it's up to the trustee to implement the regulations.

I understand the frustrations of sitting in a seat with limited power and several limitations that can make it challenging to fulfill their responsibilities effectively. The hard work for school board members is to manage these limitations. The last thing a school board needs is one or two members going rogue and disrupting the district for individual press and gains.

In a few instances, school board trustees are often unpaid volunteers, which can limit their availability and expertise. Many trustees have other jobs and commitments, making it difficult to dedicate sufficient time and energy to their role. While trustees may bring diverse perspectives and experiences to the table, they may need to gain specific expertise and training to make informed decisions about complex educational issues. I will repeat myself, one of the best investments a school board can make is in the constant training of the trustee. One can never learn enough.

Non-Partisan Seat

Depending on the platform they choose when campaigning, school board trustees may face challenges maintaining positive relationships with other stakeholders in their district, including parents, teachers, and community members. Different groups may have competing priorities or perspectives and it can be challenging for trustees to balance these interests while making decisions that benefit the district.

The last few years have seen a shift in the American body politic. It has become caustic, mean, and downright ugly. Unfortunately, the national trend has seeped into school board races. The article, *A Nonpartisan Model for Developing Public Service Leadership*, published in the Harvard Business Review in April 2020, suggests a new approach to developing public service leadership.

The article suggests that current leadership development programs often prioritize political ideology over practical skills and experience, resulting in leaders who need more expertise to tackle complex public issues.

At the County Building accepting my oath of office of run for office

The authors argue that a nonpartisan approach to leadership development would better prepare leaders to address complex challenges. They propose a four-stage model for nonpartisan leadership development.

- First, selecting individuals with diverse backgrounds and experiences

- Second, providing training in both practical skills and leadership competencies
- Third, engaging participants in a variety of hands-on experiences to gain real-world experience
- And fourth, providing ongoing support and mentorship to reinforce leadership skills.

Why School Board Races Should Remain Nonpartisan, is a 2017 article by Michael Holzman, that was published in the Washington Post. The article argues that nonpartisan school board races ensure that candidates prioritize the interests of students rather than their party affiliation and maintain a focus on improving education for all students.

Nonpartisan school board races ensure that candidates prioritize students' interests and focus on improving education for all students. They prevent political polarization and promote cooperation and collaboration among school board members, improving student educational outcomes. Additionally, nonpartisan school board races prevent candidates from being defined by their party affiliation and promote a focus on education policy.

The risks associated with bringing personal politics into non-partisan school board seats highlight the negative impacts on students, the erosion of trust within the community, and the potential for biased decision-making. Each of us has our own personal politics, but inserting personal politics into non-partisan school board seats can divert attention from the primary goal of providing quality education. Instead of focusing on policies, initiatives, and curricula that benefit students, board members may prioritize advancing their own political agenda, which hinders educational progress and detracts from the board's ability to make objective decisions.

Incorporating personal politics into non-partisan school board seats often increases the community's polarization and divisiveness. School boards are meant to bring people together to address educational challenges collectively. However, when personal political ideologies are injected into the equation, it can create an "us versus them" mentality, deepening divisions among board members, parents, and community stakeholders.

I believe in the case of school board trustees, this nonpartisan approach to leadership development is essential to developing influential, public service leaders. By prioritizing practical skills and real-world experience, nonpartisan leadership development programs can prepare leaders to tackle complex public issues and promote positive change in their communities.

Lighthouse Study

In March 2017, The Iowa Association of School Boards, with the support of the National School Boards Association, conducted ongoing research on effective school boards and their roles in advancing student achievement.

In recent months I have witnessed many school boards and superintendent relationships become more contentious than at any other time in my tenure. It's not just my observation. One can pick up a newspaper and read about the firing of a superintendent over politically charged issues, from book banning and curriculum issues to lack of student performance. I've heard that the average tenure of a superintendent is less than seven years on the job.

The relationship between a school board and superintendent is critical to the success of a school district. A strong partnership between the school board and superintendent can lead to better decision-making, more effective use of resources, and improved student educational outcomes. School Boards are responsible for district success, but they cannot do it alone. They must hire, assign responsibility to, and delegate authority to, someone who can lead the staff on a day-to-day basis. (Maloney, 2023) By working collaboratively, they can establish a shared vision, make effective decisions, build trust and communication, and improve student achievement.

Because the school board has the power to hire, evaluate, and fire them, superintendents have good reason to tread cautiously and steer clear of potential conflicts with the board. Many in the role walk the tightrope, wondering if they antagonized board members in any way, stirred up controversies, or made unpopular decisions. In that case, they know their performance ratings and job security may suffer (White & Linberg, 2021). Here is where each party should work together to establish clear goals and priorities and develop a shared understanding of success. Working toward a common goal can create a strong sense of purpose and unity within the district.

School boards can create conditions that promote student learning. In a paper presented to the American Educational Research Association, the Iowa Lighthouse Inquiry research team reported on the behaviors of the school board/superintendent dynamic among districts with extreme differences in student achievement. The research provided key findings concerning the characteristics of effective school boards and differences in the behaviors of effective and less effective boards.

Studies have identified the characteristics of school boards with higher levels of student achievement and how they lead their districts toward high performance. School board actions are a crucial part of a "culture of improvement." The school board and superintendent must be aligned in their vision for the district.

Effective school board relationships with the boards and the superintendents shared key attributes and indicators, as follows:

- Peaceful relationships—The board/superintendent teams had relatively amicable relationships. Typically, board members in all studied districts said, "We disagree without making it personal."
- Board opinions of the superintendents—All boards were reasonably satisfied with their superintendents.
- Caring about children—While their specific behaviors and attitudes were remarkably different, in all cases the people interviewed appeared to care deeply about doing the right thing for children.

I have been blessed to work with three outstanding superintendents: Kip Hearron, Kevin Silberberg, and Katie Russell. The relationship between a school board and superintendent is critical and sacred to the success of a school district. These two groups of leaders work together to set the vision and direction of the district, make important decisions, and ensure that students receive a high-quality education. Here are some reasons this relationship is so meaningful:

1. Shared Vision: The school board and superintendent must work together to establish a shared vision for the district. The superintendent is responsible for implementing the board's policies and initiatives, and the board must support the superintendent's efforts to improve student achievement. When both groups are on the same page, they can create a cohesive strategy that will lead to positive student outcomes.

2. Effective Decision-Making: The school board and

superintendent must work together to make sound decisions for the district. The board sets policies and approves budgets, while the superintendent oversees the district's day-to-day operations. By working collaboratively, they can ensure that decisions are made with the best interests of students in mind.

3. Trust and Communication: Open communication and trust are essential to a successful school board and superintendent relationship. When both groups have a good working relationship, they can engage in honest, open dialogue and address issues before they become major problems. They can also work together to build trust with stakeholders in the community, including teachers, parents, and students.

4. Student Achievement: Ultimately, the success of the school board/superintendent relationship is reflected in student achievement. When working together effectively, both groups can create a district-wide culture of high expectations and academic excellence. This can increase student achievement, improve graduation rates, and better student outcomes.

One key factor in building a successful school board-superintendent relationship is communication. There have been times when my superintendent and I were not on the same page. I recall a time when the same-sex bathroom was an issue, and there was a meeting about school boundary changes (there is no heated meeting like one in which boundary change is discussed). Kevin, and I disagreed on which one to tackle. He has his viewpoint, and I held mine. After a rigorous discussion and between three bottles of water, Kevin and I came to an agreement. Well not actually, his case made more sense than mine and well....he was correct.

I believe we got through this because of the constant and regular communication between us. There was, and still is a mutual respect for each of our values and competency. While there was disagreement we both wanted the best for our stakeholders and we kept this in the forefront. I had to remember he is there 60 hours a week and has a better picture than I do. This is where I had to close my mouth and open my ears. It was an open and transparent conversation which was the key to moving forward as a governance team.

The reason my board is one of the better ones in the state of California and the nation is because of an essential factor: mutual respect between the trustees and the district staff. Does this suggest we have always agreed on every issue? Absolutely not! Yet, we have worked really hard to understand each respective roles and responsibilities and respect each other's expertise and perspectives. By working together as partners, we can leverage our strengths and ensure the district moves in the right direction.

The Gift of Words

Sometimes the relationship between the superintendent and the trustee becomes personal and life-changing. We were returning from San Francisco after attending the annual CSBA (California School Boards Association) conference. Kevin Silberberg, my superintendent, was driving, I was in the passenger seat, and his wife, Dawn, was in the second row of the SUV. Kevin's wife was asking him what the family should do for Christmas.

Dawn offered various suggestions going back and forth, while a heavy rainstorm got heavier along with traffic. I would tell Kevin that the combination of weather, traffic, and parts of the conversion were taking their toll on his nerves. Their discussion of options lasted for about twenty-five minutes, while Kevin, either out of frustration or brilliance, said, "You know what? Just have the gift of words." Dawn Silberberg paused, waited a minute or so, and said with peace of mind in her voice, "Yes, that will do."

The gift of words? This was a new idea for me, and I wondered to myself what that meant. While staring out the window trying to determine what this gift of words thing was. Sheepishly, I got the courage to ask Kevin, "What's the gift of words?"

What Kevin and Dawn didn't know was that my family was on the verge of falling apart. Life was kicking me in the butt. I didn't have money for Christmas gifts for my family. During that year, if anything could go wrong for me--it did. Whatever plans I made professionally, plummeted. Money was extremely tight, creditors were calling, and my hope for a brighter and better future was fading fast.

I was flat on my back, worse than Fraizer after the 1973 knockout loss to George Foremen. Both of them explained that their family tradition every Christmas Eve is that during the gift exchange portion, instead of exchanging presents, you tell each other how much you love or appreciate them. I thought to myself, "My goodness, how beautiful," but it would never work in the Wolaridge household, especially after the year we were having.

As we crossed the Altamont Pass, I sat silent and said to myself, "The gift of words. It's a risk. The girls are expecting gifts, but I will try it." Three weeks later, as per our family tradition, we had the traditional Secret Santa Christmas Eve, finger foods, homemade nacho dip, eggrolls, and buffalo chicken wings. With the fireplace roaring in the background, the six of us gathered together in our circle. While I earned enough money for one gift per person, I mustered up the courage, introduced the gift of words, and modeled how it would work. For my Secret Santa, I gave my token of love to my daughter and took another minute to tell her how much I loved and appreciated her for who she was. This surprised my family.

Next, the one who just received her gift gave her Secret Santa gift to her sister and followed it with her gift of words. This went on for six rounds. Hearing the words of affection and adoration we had for one another, tears filled my wife's and my eyes. Thanks to Silberberg's, they gave us a gift that money can never purchase. They gave me my family's unity back. The gift of words is now a standing Christmas Eve tradition in the Wolaridge household that will be passed on from generation to generation. I will forever be thankful and grateful to Kevin and Dawn Silberberg.

I'm not suggesting in my story that trustees and superintendents have this type of personal moment to get the work done, but I have concluded that the school board/superintendent relationship is critical to effective school governance. By building a solid partnership based on communication, mutual respect, and a shared vision for the district, trustees and superintendents can work together to improve educational outcomes for all students.

No Individual Authority

The reality of serving on a school board can be very different from what one imagines, even for new board members who have studied the board's functions and attended numerous board meetings before running for office. Serving on a school board will stretch and develop one's leadership abilities, just like any demanding leadership position. Schools aim to give our kids access to quality educational opportunities.

Keeping this in mind, upholding the rule that students' interests and academic achievement should always come first in all board decisions, and member actions is crucial. Due to the wide range of requests for actions and decisions from various constituencies, this is frequently a challenging task.

A fundamental rule for those wishing to become board members is that no one has personal authority to act on behalf of the school board or the district. Only the school board as a whole and the singular entity can act or exercise school board authority. Each board member is given the authority to speak and vote on each matter when the meeting is called to order.

Only a majority of the board can set policy, establish the school district budget, negotiate contracts, or make requests to the superintendent. The only employee of the board and the only person to whom the board may make requests in the school district is the superintendent.

As a trustee, you must understand that the school district's leadership group is comprised of the board and the superintendent. This does not imply that everyone agrees on the problems or the most effective solution. In fact, rational school board decision-making depends on a healthy debate.

Discussions about important topics for a team that works well and has high trust will be heated and passionate. The board will support its decisions because of their shared trust. Respecting the principle of majority rule is essential to efficient school board management. Doing otherwise, the team's effectiveness cannot be improved, and the board's standing among the staff and community generally declines.

The I "Mindset."

The "I" mentality is often emphasized and rewarded in today's society. Many individuals are focused on personal success, often at the expense of others. This mentality is prevalent in our culture, from how we talk about achievement to how we structure our organizations. In our society, success is often defined as individual achievements, such as being the top performer in a given field, receiving promotions, and earning high salaries. This emphasis on individual achievement can create a culture that values competition over collaboration, which can ultimately be detrimental to the district's success.

Bill George's (2015) book, *Discover Your True North,* outlines his philosophy on leadership, which he believes involves looking inward and discovering one's authentic self. One of the most important aspects of his philosophy is the shift from an "I" to a "we" mentality. This shift emphasizes the importance of teamwork and collaboration in achieving success rather than individual achievement.

The "We" Mentality

Bill George argues that the "we" mentality is a more effective approach to leadership. This mentality emphasizes the importance of collaboration, teamwork, and shared goals. In a "we" culture, the team's success is the primary goal, rather than individual achievement. This type of culture fosters a sense of community and can lead to increased motivation, productivity, and job satisfaction.

As a school board member, shifting from an "I" to a "we" mentality requires conscious effort. It starts with you sharing, creating, and collaborating on a shared vision and goal that everyone can work toward. In his latest book, *The 16 Undeniable Laws Of Communication*, Dr. John Maxwell (2023) references *How Successful People Think* and summarizes why collaboration is so highly valued and necessary for organizational growth.

He states:

- Shared thinking is faster than solo thinking
- Shared thinking brings more maturity than solo thinking
- Shared thinking is more creative than solo thinking
- Shared thinking is the only way to have great thinking

This vision should be communicated clearly and reviewed regularly so that each governance team member is on the same page. Great thoughts are born of many good thoughts and shared thinking returns greater value than solo thinking. Dr. Maxwell continues that in his many years of speaking and leading, he learned that "success or failure is not determined by the weight of what you need to accomplish or the heaviness of the load you carry. It's determined by the people you collaborate with to help you accomplish the task." (p 93)

School board members that embrace a trusting mindset benefit the district and community. In *The Infinite Game*, Simon Sinek (2019), explains that there is a difference between a group of people who work together and a group of people who trust each other. In a group of people who simply work together, relationships are mostly transactional, based on a mutual desire to get things done.

When we work on a trusting team, we feel safe to express vulnerability. We feel safe raising our hands and admitting we made a mistake, being honest about shortfalls in performance, taking responsibility for our behavior, and asking for help. From my experience, the most significant benefit is that it can increase motivation and productivity when doing the work.

It has been my experience that our trustee team pulled together; each of us felt like we were part of a team and that our contributions were valued, so we were more likely to be engaged and committed to our work. In turn, it fostered a sense of community working together toward a shared goal. We developed a sense of camaraderie and mutual respect, which led to better decision-making and created a positive work environment and model for the district.

Provide and Protect

The community may vote you into office because of your qualifications and feel you will do what is best for their most important asset: their child. For me, as a trustee, I must remember this at all times: *I am a trustee of the tax dollar and someone's child. In a nutshell.* "School governance" is simply corporate governance in a school setting.

In his book, *The Art of School Boarding*, Jim Burgett (2013) summarizes the three primary goals of effective school governance: accountability, fairness, and transparency. One must comprehend the meaning and guiding principles of "governance" to serve as a school board trustee. "Corporate governance" refers to the set of policies and procedures that a board of directors uses to ensure that a company interacts fairly and openly with all its stakeholders.

"Corporate governance" is that framework of rules and practices by which a board of trustees ensures accountability, fairness, and transparency in a company's relationship with its stakeholders. This involves acting to exemplify the district's values, goals, and vision and providing resources that support mutually agreed-upon priorities and objectives, as well as upholding district policies the board has approved and maintaining the board-approved district policies. It means ensuring that a positive personnel climate exists and being knowledgeable enough about district efforts to explain them to the public.

Strategic Direction

One of the primary responsibilities of board members is to provide strategic direction for the organization. Members are responsible for setting the organization's overall direction, including its mission, vision, and values. Board members need to understand the external environment and assess the organization's strengths, weaknesses, opportunities, and threats to make decisions about the organization's priorities and goals.

As a trustee, one should ensure that the organization's strategic direction aligns with its mission and vision. They must set clear goals and objectives and develop strategies to achieve them. Board members should regularly review and update the organization's strategic plan to remain relevant and practical.

Effective strategic direction is crucial for the success of the district. It helps to ensure that the organization is moving in the right direction, is responsive to changes in the external environment, and is focused on achieving its goals and objectives.

Financial Oversight

Another critical role of school board members is to provide financial oversight for the organization. They are responsible for ensuring that the organization is financially sustainable and that its resources are effectively used. This involves reviewing and approving budgets, monitoring financial performance, and confirming that the organization complies with relevant laws and regulations.

You and your fellow trustees will oversee millions of taxpayer dollars. In addition to creating good policies, the budget is the school board's primary area of oversight and this is a huge responsibility. The board makes financial decisions that best serve kids' needs and promotes development. The board must monitor the performance of invested funds and allocate budgetary funds.

It would be best if you funded the programs important to your school. ***And that may mean saying no to adults***. This is not easy, but if you keep the district's vision, mission, and values, know what the key results are that you'd like to see for the money spent---and hold the district accountable.

The more effective trustees spend time with the Chief Business Officer, CBO, and ask questions to understand the three budgets that a district works with concurrently. A trustee's job is to monitor, work with the business department, and take corrective action should financial circumstances change.

Risk Management

Along with the superintendent, board members are responsible for identifying and managing organizational risks. Many times, this deals with lawsuits that arise within the organization. School districts have insurance coverage to cover any potential losses.

Still, the board is there to advise the superintendent in the areas of operational, legal, strategic, and reputational risks. Here is where your wisdom as a trustee is needed. Be prepared for that unexpected phone call, text, or email from your superintendent who is preparing you for unexpected events, ensuring that a procedure is in place and the organization's reputation is protected.

**Proud to have served as Board President for two consecutive years
2016 – 2018**

On the next few pages, let's discover the four, Core Duties of school board members.

The Big Four

1. The Duty of Care

Fiduciary duty requires board members to stay objective, unselfish, responsible, honest, trustworthy, and efficient. As stewards of public trust, board members must always act for the organization's good rather than for their own benefit. They must exercise reasonable care in all decision-making without putting the organization at unnecessary risk.

Duty of Care refers to a fiduciary responsibility held by company directors, requiring them to live up to a standard of care. This duty requires them to make decisions in good faith and a reasonably prudent manner. These people must exercise the utmost care in making business decisions to fulfill their fiduciary duty.

In 2000, *The Ethical Obligations of School Board Members*, by the National School Board Association emphasized the ethical responsibilities of school board members and their duty of obedience to the law. The article outlined various ethical principles and standards of behavior that board members should adhere to, including acting in the best interest of students, being transparent and accountable, avoiding conflicts of interest, and respecting the rights of others. It also discusses the importance of maintaining confidentiality and upholding professional standards.

The Duty of Care describes the level of competence expected of a board member. In education, the duty of care requires teachers and school administrators to provide students with a safe and secure environment. This includes taking reasonable steps to prevent bullying, harassment, and violence, and providing appropriate supervision and training.

It is commonly expressed as the Duty of Care that "an ordinarily, prudent person would exercise in a like position and under similar circumstances." This means that a board member is responsible for exercising reasonable care when deciding on a steward of the organization. It does not mean that you have to be perfect or that you cannot make a mistake. Instead, it means that you have exercised reasonable caution in making decisions. Ways to exercise the duty of care include:

• Be informed (the duty is to learn about the organization, its vision, mission, and initiatives; learn about its programs; read materials.)

• Attend meetings and functions (a simple way of becoming and staying informed). A failure to attend in and of itself may be considered a failure to carry out one's fiduciary responsibilities. Meetings can be conducted in person or through Zoom and phone conferences. The law has not caught up with technology, so the legality of Internet conferences is unclear. Non-attendance may or may not be protected against a board of directors' wrongful action charges. It will, in part, depend on the individual judge/court.

• To be truly protected, a vote should record your objection. Be familiar with the organization's financial status. Information flow means to: cause the organization to create and offer reports that keep the Board of Directors informed promptly and accurately. Make informed decisions. Did we seek out information? Did we ask questions and deliberate? Did I participate in discussions/deliberations?

2. The Duty of Loyalty

The duty of loyalty is a standard of faithfulness. A board member must give undivided allegiance when making decisions affecting the organization, which means that a board member must never use information gained as a board member for personal gain but must act in the organization's best interests. Adhering to this standard of duty prohibits conflicts of interest. It requires individuals to prioritize the interests of the district over their own. This duty requires school board members to act with the utmost good faith and to exercise the highest degree of care and diligence, avoiding self-dealing and other actions that could benefit them personally at the expense of the board and district.

At the time of my writing this chapter, one of my fellow board members had resigned from his seat due to this principle. My former trustee has my respect because he embodied the principle of the duty of loyalty and his personal morality and ethics.

3. The Duty of Best Interest

You will understand and/or identify with specific constituencies (parents, neighborhoods or communities, special education, etc.). Still, it would be best if you remembered that being a board member means retaining the community's trust.

There is no way your board of three to seven people can provide a spokesperson for every constituency or legitimate interest so, morally, you must stand for them all. You can be FROM a constituency, but you must not let yourself **SOLELY REPRESENT IT**. Ensure that every deliberation, decision, and action reflects the best interests of every student you serve. No child is more important than another.

As a school board member, the Duty of Best Interest is a critical, ethical, and legal obligation that requires you to act in the best interests of ALL students, staff, and the community you serve. In fulfilling their Duty of Best Interest, school board members must also be aware of, and comply with all applicable laws, regulations, and policies. This includes federal and state laws related to education, civil rights, and other relevant areas.

The best available evidence, research, and professional expertise must guide school board members' decisions to uphold the Best Interest Duty. Board members must be well-informed and knowledgeable about education policy, curriculum, school finance, and school safety, among other topics. They must also be aware of the needs and interests of the students, staff, and community they serve, and consider these factors when making decisions.

This is my personal opinion, but the Best Interest Duty also includes a responsibility to promote equity, diversity, and inclusion in the schools and communities that school board members serve. This means that board members must work to eliminate any forms of discrimination or bias in school policies, practices, and curricula. They must also strive to ensure that all students have equal access to educational opportunities and resources, regardless of their background, identity, or socioeconomic status.

4. The Duty of Obedience

The Texas Association of School Boards provided an article, A *Guide to Ethical Decision-Making for School Board Members*, which guides school board members on making ethical decisions and fulfilling their Duty of Obedience. As a school board member, making ethical decisions is a crucial part of fulfilling your role in maintaining the integrity of the educational system. One of the critical principles in ethical decision-making requires that school board members comply with all applicable laws and regulations, and act by the school district's policies and procedures.

I am reminded of the time when I was first elected, and I thought I could rule the world from my seat at the dais. I remember having an idea and I made an appointment and privately talked with my superintendent about the change I wanted to make in the district. After he listened, he smiled and told me to turn around. When I looked behind me, a shelf of books stretched horizontally from eight to ten feet. This lexicon turned out to be the entire California Educational Code. He said my ideas made some sense, but they were against the rules in those books.

This was a lesson on why board members should stay informed about the laws and regulations governing their school district and participate in training sessions to deepen their understanding of ethical decision-making.

Board members should also strive to be transparent in their decision-making processes by communicating with stakeholders and keeping accurate records of all deliberations. Failure to comply with this duty can result in legal and financial liabilities, damage to the school board's reputation, and harm to the students, staff, and community that the board serves. This guide also underscores the importance of avoiding conflicts of interest and ensuring that all decision-making processes are fair and impartial.

This can be difficult, but the Duty of Obedience requires school board members to comply with all decisions made by the board or its designated authorities. This includes decisions related to the adoption of policies, the approval of budgets, the selection of personnel, and other matters related to the operation and governance of the school district. Even if you disagree with state law, the duty of obedience requires that a school board trustee works to ensure that the organization complies with applicable laws and regulations, follows its policies, and carries out its mission appropriately.

Board members must also comply with decisions about legal issues, such as lawsuits or other legal actions brought against the district. Board members should ensure that the organization carries out its purpose and does not engage in unauthorized activities.

I will repeat myself. The system's heart and soul are the board of education. So, they must avoid making decisions based on personal biases or agendas and must act in a manner that promotes the overall goals and objectives of the school district.

School board members do not hold administrative positions in the way that directors or superintendents do. They are elected representatives of the public tasked with overseeing and directing the school district with regard to organization, strategic planning, operations, finances, and student achievement. Which means this school board members respect the authority and autonomy of the superintendent and other district administrators. There are countless examples where school board members violate this principle.

Working on behalf of students across the state

While the trustee may mean well, overstepping one's implicit or implied authority can cause issues and problems. It may be difficult for a few, but board members must avoid micromanaging or interfering with the school district's day-to-day operations. The key is to trust the expertise and judgment of district administrators and support them where necessary.

Reflective Questions - Chapter 2

1. In the context of serving on a school board, how might the shift from an "I" to a "we" mentality, as advocated by Bill George, impact decision-making processes and relationships within the board? How can embracing a collaborative mindset contribute to the effective management of a school board?

2. Considering the "Duty of Best Interest" outlined for school board members, how can trustees balance the diverse interests and constituencies within a community while ensuring that every decision aligns with the best interests of all students, staff, and the community? What challenges might arise in fulfilling this duty, and how can they be addressed?

3. The text emphasizes the importance of the "Duty of Obedience" for school board members, requiring compliance with laws, regulations, and decisions made by the board. How can trustees navigate situations where their personal ideas conflict with existing laws or regulations, and how might transparency and communication play a role in ethical decision-making within a school board?

Chapter 3

The Learning Journey Begins. Leaving a Lasting Legacy on the Educational Community

———————⌒———————

Whether or not we are school board trustees, embracing lifelong learning is essential as we progress through life. I firmly believe in encouraging others to try new things and learn new skills.

The term 'lifelong learning' refers to acquiring knowledge, skills, and competencies throughout one's life. It starts from early childhood until the end of one's life. Being a lifelong learner means being open to new ideas, challenges, and experiences that will help us grow, develop, and thrive. One of my fellow trustees told me that school board members must be the district's top students. Many states have training requirements for school board members. By statute in Pennsylvania, every new board member is now required to attend five hours of training upon being elected to the school board.

In today's fast-paced world, where technology and innovation constantly transform our society, being a lifelong learner in education has become increasingly important. Advances in science, technology, and social norms profoundly impact our lives, and it's only through lifelong learning that we can stay up to date with these changes. With new technologies being developed and launched rapidly, learning new skills and competencies is critical to staying relevant and knowledgeable.

As a trustee and/or board member, you must invest time in learning this craft. This learning can take many forms, from formal education to workshops, classes, conferences, and self-directed learning. In many districts, those who have been reelected are required to attend three hours of training. (Panza, 2023) We always need to be fully informed. We don't know everything, regardless of who we are---and there's always something new to learn.

In California, school board formal education provided by The California School Board Association (CSBA) has structured programs that lead to a degree or certification with a Master's in Governance (MIG) and I am a proud 2016 graduate. There is also self-directed learning that involves learning through various sources, such as books, professional journals, online resources, and practical experiences. Each form of learning is equally important and can help us acquire knowledge and skills essential for being an informed school board member.

Cedric Crawford (2015), Mr. Make it Great, in his book *Breadcrumbs To Making It Great Volume 2,* makes the case that if we know better, *we should do better!* I agree with Cedric when he writes, "Our quest for knowledge should be never-ending, like an unquenchable thirst and unsatisfiable hunger." He continues, "I know enough to know that I don't know nearly enough and will always need to know more."(p.193)

I gave remarks at the countywide school board trustee meeting

In today's rapidly changing educational and cultural landscape, trustees must possess, and constantly develop, a growth mindset, which means we are open to new challenges and willing to take risks to educate our students. This will differ from school district to school district. Only you know what your community's needs are. Still, it's up to you as a trustee to understand all sides of an issue before making decisions. They must adapt to changes in technology, curriculum, and instructional methods. Therefore, lifelong learning assists in staying current in this area. I believe the best trustees are those who cultivate a mindset of curiosity and a thirst for knowledge.

We should be open to new ideas and experiences and be willing to challenge our existing beliefs and assumptions. We should also be willing to take risks and try new things, even when we don't know if we will succeed. Learning from failure is an essential part of the lifelong learning process, and we should embrace it as *an opportunity to grow and develop.*

Am I recommending reckless abandon in our children's education? By no means. But I am asking that, as a trustee, you step back, challenge your assumptions, and see the other side of the coin. Invest the time to learn all you can about school finance, maintenance, instructional services, curriculum, special education; so forth and so on. This will take some time, but you don't have to do it alone. To make good decisions for the kids in the district, you must learn about the district and all the nuances that accompany it.

With the internet and other tools out there, so much is available to you and that's what's so great! You have no excuse. It always makes me crazy when I run into someone who replies, "Nah, nah, nah, I got it." That is not the way we should ever think. You become more innovative and challenged by continuing to learn throughout your life. You never know what doors it might open for you. You might come across an idea from another district or trustee that may positively affect your district. That might lead you in a different direction, but that's alright.

Blind Spots

We all have blind spots within our schools, in ourselves--- not to mention in our ability to govern. If we are upfront and honest, there are things we mistakenly believe we are already doing well but are actually doing awfully. Most people think of their blind spots as weaknesses, but that's not what a blind spot is.

Dr. Lucia Vazquez, Director of the California Latino School Boards Association and former Trustee for Visalia Unified School District speaks of the blind spots of leaders and community leaders regarding marginalized populations. "The poor, marginalized communities that most need supplies, technology, internet access, meals, and transportation were overlooked" (Guilliam 2020). Vasquez mentions time and time again that she heard from colleagues that wealthier parents were blind to the fact that there are high-needs schools. She marvels that in other districts during the pandemic, the poorest schools were often left out of the distribution of resources. At the time, this was an immense blind spot for her district.

No district is perfect and each one has its issues. However, many school board members get into trouble because they act like their district doesn't have any problems. Here are two essential virtues that will serve you well in the seat: honesty and humility. In her book *Rookie Smarts*, Liz Wisemen (2014) makes the case that the most dangerous place in the world might be at the top, whether it's the top of the ladder or at the top of your game. Bill Gates said, "Success is a lousy teacher; it seduces smart people into thinking they can't lose." (Bryant, 2016) Experience plus hubris make for a lousy combination.

Every district has blind spots. When you don't see what's there, it's like strolling around with food in your teeth with great confidence until you approach a mirror and see it yourself. Then comes the embarrassment and pain, but you take steps to remove it. The same is true for your school district. If it means hearing unfavorable comments about the district in the feedback from parents and community members, it's your responsibility as a trustee to safeguard and support your district. You should want this critique and welcome it! I can assure you that no matter what the district does, you have blind spots.

As a trustee, if you haven't been told something humbling and unexpected about your district, it is that blind spot that prevents your schools from going to the next level. Remember this, when a man whose marriage was in trouble sought advice, the Master said, "You must learn to listen to your wife." After a month, the man took this advice to heart and returned to say he had learned to listen to every word his wife was saying. Said the Master with a smile, "Now go home and listen to every word she isn't saying."

A blind spot is a gap or weakness in understanding ourselves, others, or situations, believe it or not, you have blind spots in your governance abilities and acumen. Overcoming personal blind spots is essential to personal and professional growth. Biases, limited experiences, or a lack of self-awareness can cause these gaps or weaknesses. For many of you reading this book, this may be the first time you have considered becoming an elected official. So, the assumption is that---you don't know what you don't know. Here is where self-examination and maturity come into play.

This role may be similar to your previous experience, but it's not the same. As a school board member, you are part of a governance team. This means *the team* makes collective decisions for the children in your district. While you may have your personal preferences, dogmas, or beliefs, they have little to do with team governance.

Early in my tenure, I held strong personal beliefs that I felt were best for the district. I advocated for them whenever I could. Yet the direction of the district is not up to one individual. It's the responsibility of the entire board. For many, this is a rude awakening. The current political climate may give one a false sense of importance and authority. Don't let the examples we have witnessed over the last few years get you into trouble for overstepping your authority.

This may ruffle feathers for some and irritate others, but I must state it here. For some, governance and authority will expose your blind spots. If you were insecure before being elected, being elected will increase your insecurities. If you have an unquenchable need to be heard, being given a microphone and an audience will lay bare your deep-seated need. If you are not careful or challenged, you may abuse your perceived power. If having no agency or authority as a child was an issue, as an adult with some authority, this role will uncover your deep-seated need to be in charge, and your superintendent and staff will bear the weight. As the saying goes, "What is in the wash will come out in the rinse." Your district doesn't need you to use the office to meet some unmet needs as an adolescent. If this is your case, please work these issues out before considering serving. If you believe this isn't you, take heed lest you fall.

Since we all have personal blind spots, here are some strategies to overcome them:

- Developing keen self-awareness is the foundation of personal growth. It helps us identify our strengths, weaknesses, biases, and values. Self-awareness enables us to recognize our blind spots and work on them. Self-reflection, journaling, and seeking feedback from others can help us develop self-awareness.

- Seeking feedback from others can help us identify our blind spots. Feedback can come from various sources, such as mentors, colleagues, friends, and family.

It's important to seek input from trustworthy people who have our best interests at heart.

- We must challenge our assumptions. This isn't easy, but our assumptions can limit our understanding of situations and others. It's essential to challenge our assumptions and consider other perspectives. We can do this by seeking diverse viewpoints and listening actively to others. I have had to embrace the idea that learning from others can help us broaden our perspectives and overcome our blind spots. We can learn from others by reading books, attending workshops, and conversing with people from diverse backgrounds.

- Empathy is yet another good practice. Empathy helps us connect with others and better understand their perspectives. Practicing empathy can help us overcome our blind spots by enabling us to see situations from different angles.

For trustees to be at their best to serve their districts, overcoming personal blind spots requires putting in the work. By working on our blind spots, we can become more effective school board members, community leaders, communicators, and collaborators. We can also develop a deeper understanding of ourselves and others, leading to greater personal and professional fulfillment.

Stay Curious

A favorite quote of mine is by Mark Twain. He states, "It ain't what you don't know that gets you into trouble; it's what you know for sure that just ain't so." Unfortunately, many school board members walk around and get comfortable, thinking we know everything and have all the answers.   -

Curiosity is the innate human tendency to seek knowledge,

understanding, and novelty. It drives us to ask questions, explore the world, and discover new things. Staying curious is essential for personal growth, intellectual development, and progress in various aspects of life. For some, the true tenets of our business may translate to education, and some will not.

Good school board members are always curious. The best members ask questions not to show how smart they are but to seek and discover the best answers. Trustees often have the attitude of "we've tried that" or "done it." If you still have this problem, one indication is that you didn't ask the right questions. Better trustees always look for solutions to their district's issues. There is nothing wrong with getting help from outside resources such as seminars, conferences, and conversations with other school board members.

Curiosity Fosters Learning

Staying curious fosters learning, encouraging us to seek new knowledge and ideas. When we are curious, we ask questions, conduct research (not Google searching) and seek answers.

For example, John Dewey, an American philosopher, psychologist, and educational reformer, believed in the importance of active learning, critical thinking, and integrating education with real-life experiences. Dewey's curious thinking and progressive ideas influenced educational theory and practice, promoting the concept of "learning by doing" and advocating for education that addresses students' needs and interests. His philosophy continues to significantly impact educational systems worldwide, emphasizing the development of students' problem-solving abilities and democratic values.

This learning process enables us to expand our knowledge,

broaden our horizons, and enhance our intellectual skills. Additionally, staying curious enhances our ability to adapt to change, allowing us to acquire new skills and knowledge in response to evolving situations.

Curiosity Fuels Creativity

Curiosity fuels creativity by encouraging us to think outside the box and explore new ideas. One of my favorites is the example of Marva Collins. Ms. Collins was an influential educator known for her transformative impact on the lives of disadvantaged students. Her approach to education, centered around high expectations, rigorous academics, and a nurturing environment, challenged prevailing beliefs about the capabilities of marginalized, primarily Black children. Collins founded the Westside Preparatory School in Chicago in 1975, mainly serving African American students from low-income backgrounds. Her educational philosophy rejected the notion that poverty or a challenging environment should hinder academic achievement. Instead, she believed that a strong foundation in basic skills, a focus on character development, and a belief in the limitless potential of her students were vital to unlocking their success.

Collins created a stimulating and nurturing classroom environment, fostering a sense of self-worth and instilling a love for learning in her students. She emphasized personalized instruction, employing various teaching methods to cater to individual learning styles. Collins' curriculum was rigorous and comprehensive, including literature, mathematics, and the classics. She also incorporated art, music, and field trips to enrich her students' educational experiences.

The impact of Marva Collins' approach was remarkable. Students labeled "unteachable" or "at-risk" thrived under her guidance.

Many of her students went on to achieve academic success and pursue higher education. Collins' methods gained recognition and attracted attention from educators worldwide, leading to numerous accolades and invitations to share her insights on effective teaching.

Through her dedication and innovative teaching methods, Collins empowered students and showed that every child has the potential to succeed. Her direct impact on students inspired a generation of educators and parents to believe in the possibility of all children. Her legacy is a reminder that with dedication, high expectations, and a nurturing environment, educational barriers can be overcome and that every child can flourish.

Curiosity Encourages Exploration

Staying curious encourages exploration and motivates us to seek new experiences and ideas. Paulo Freire was a Brazilian educator and philosopher renowned for his critical pedagogy work. Freire's curious thinking centered around the transformative power of education in addressing social inequalities and promoting social justice.

Freire's (1970) seminal work, *Pedagogy of the Oppressed*, challenged traditional educational models and advocated a liberating approach to empowering marginalized individuals through dialogue, reflection, and conscientization. Freire's ideas have profoundly impacted educational theory and practice, particularly in adult education and education for social change. His work inspires educators seeking to create more inclusive and equitable learning environments.

The highlights of the job are visiting classrooms where teachers like Dr. Byron Bowens show love and compassion

When curious, we are more likely to explore unfamiliar territories, meet new people, and try new things. This exploration process can be enlightening, as it exposes us to different cultures, ideas, and ways of thinking.

Curiosity Enhances Problem-Solving Abilities

The ability to be curious is the ability to learn and grow in understanding the world and one's place in it. It's fundamental to school board leadership. Curious trustees enhance our problem-solving abilities, encouraging us to seek solutions to complex problems.

When curious, we ask questions, seek out information, and evaluate different options. Using this approach as a trustee allows us to develop critical thinking skills, analytical abilities, and creativity. Curiosity helps us approach problems with an open mind, allowing us to explore unconventional solutions.

Curiosity Stimulates Innovation

Staying curious stimulates innovation, encouraging us to explore new ideas and push boundaries. When we are interested, we challenge existing concepts, experiment with new ideas, and seek unconventional solutions.

You may be familiar with Maria Montessori. Maria Montessori was an Italian physician and educator who developed the Montessori method of education. Her curious thinking and observations of children's learning behaviors led her to develop an innovative approach emphasizing independence, freedom within limits, and hands-on learning.

Montessori's approach revolutionized early childhood education, emphasizing individualized instruction and creating an environment that supports children's natural curiosity and desire to learn. This innovation produced progress, enabling us to develop new technologies, create new products, and advance society.

Because of 'curious thinking,' the world, for the most part, is a better place. Examples include Einstein's theory of relativity, which challenges the traditional understanding of how the universe operates and paves the way for numerous technological advancements, such as GPS systems and nuclear energy. The discovery of penicillin by Alexander Fleming's observations and investigation into the growth of bacteria ultimately led to the accidental discovery of penicillin, the world's first antibiotic, which revolutionized medicine, saving countless lives and transforming the treatment of infectious diseases.

Another example of curiosity is the development of the World Wide Web by Tim Berners-Lee. His curious thinking and desire to connect information innovatively gave rise to the World Wide Web. By developing the first web browser, he revolutionized how people share and access information, transforming communication, commerce, education, and virtually every aspect of modern life.

The above-referenced individuals changed the world and shared commonalities in their transformative impact on various fields of study. Their curious minds led to revolutionary discoveries and innovations. These individuals questioned established beliefs, challenged existing knowledge, and ultimately reshaped our understanding of the universe, medicine, information sharing, and the natural world.

For those who wish to serve as trustees, it is crucial to cultivate and maintain a curious mindset to achieve the district's goals and objectives. When school board members are intellectually interested, we are more likely to develop innovative solutions to problems, create new ideas, and think creatively. This curiosity allows us to challenge existing concepts, explore new perspectives, and create something new and unique that benefits our students and your local community.

Reflective Questions - Chapter 3

1. How can the concept of lifelong learning benefit school board members in adapting to the rapid changes in technology, education, and social norms mentioned in the text?

2. The text emphasizes the importance of self-awareness and overcoming blind spots. What strategies can a school board member employ to develop keen self-awareness and challenge their assumptions effectively?

3. In discussing the potential blind spots of school board members, the text mentions the importance of humility and honesty. How can trustees balance the need for confidence in decision-making with the humility required to acknowledge and address blind spots?

One of my campaign signs and slogans - 2018

Chapter 4

Emotional and Relational Intelligence.
Shapes Effective Governance

As a school board member Emotional intelligence (EI) is a vital aspect of effective leadership. It is the ability to recognize and understand one's emotions and use this understanding to manage relationships and influence behavior. In today's rapidly changing, complex, and emotionally charged educational environment, school board members must possess a high degree of emotional intelligence to succeed.

Pastor, author, teacher, and speaker, Dr. John Maxwell, states over and over that leadership is influence, nothing more, nothing less. In her book, *Leading with Emotional Intelligence*, author Sanela Osmic (2023) observes that emotional intelligence goes beyond traditional measures of intelligence and technical expertise.

It's inextricably linked with the components of self-awareness, self-management, social awareness, and relationship management. These qualities are vital for board directors to navigate the complexities of boardroom dynamics, build strong relationships, and make sound decisions.

Daniel Goleman is a leading figure on the topic of emotional intelligence. In his book, *Emotional Intelligence*, Goleman (1995) explores the significance of emotional intelligence in various aspects of life. He highlights that emotional intelligence is more important than IQ in determining success and well-being. Goleman emphasizes five key components of emotional intelligence: self-awareness, self-regulation, motivation, empathy, and skilled, social interactions.

Goleman posits that the skill of self-awareness is critical because it requires the ability to monitor our inner world— our thoughts, feelings, and beliefs—so that we can accurately understand ourselves and our impact on others. In writing about EI, Elaine Houston summarizes Goleman (2019) in her article, *The Importance of Emotional Intelligence,* stating, "Emotional intelligence is the ability to sense, understand and effectively apply the power and acumen of emotions as a source of human energy, information, connection, and influence."

Emotional intelligence plays a crucial role in school board work. Establishing positive relationships facilitates effective communication, empathy, and understanding, which in turn fosters stronger connections and reduces conflicts. It has been my experience that trustees with high emotional intelligence are better equipped to manage stress, collaborate with others, and exhibit leadership qualities. They also display greater adaptability, resilience, and problem-solving skills.

Earlier this year, I was reading David Walton's (2012) book, *Emotional Intelligence: A Practical Guide*, which delves into the practical aspects of EI and its application in everyday life. Walton provides insights and strategies for developing and harnessing emotional intelligence for personal and professional growth. He emphasizes that emotional intelligence is the ability to recognize and understand emotions in oneself and others and manage them effectively. He argues, just like Goleman, that EI is crucial for navigating social interactions, building strong relationships, and achieving success in various areas of life.

Leaders with high EI recognize and regulate their emotions and understand how they affect their behavior and decision-making. When not appropriately managed---chaos arises and one only has to watch the news. The topic of what and how to educate kids can become highly emotional. There are newspaper and magazine articles, and YouTube videos where boardrooms are ripped apart when discussing what or how to instruct children. It has gotten so bad that a Nevada school board member said he had thoughts of suicide before stepping down amid threats and harassment. In Virginia, a board member resigned over what she saw as politics driving decisions on masks, and the vitriol at board meetings in Wisconsin had one member fearing he would find his tires slashed. (Thompson, 2021)

Over the past few years, there has been an increase in various parts of the nation where school board meetings got out of hand because the adults could not manage their emotions. Reports of disruptive behavior, shouting matches, verbal clashes, and even physical altercations have made it challenging for the board to maintain order and conduct productive discussions.

Conflict is inevitable. It will occur in any team or organization and can be challenging to resolve. There will be times as a school board member when you and your colleagues disagree on various agenda items, and possessing a high degree of emotional intelligence is essential to managing conflict. Therefore, the first person one must govern is themselves. School board trustees with high emotional intelligence can facilitate constructive conversations that lead to positive outcomes for the district, and instances such as the one described above can oftentimes be avoided.

You might be thinking to yourself that applying emotional intelligence is easier said than done. I get it. Managing your emotions, especially when the situation gets heated is tough as a trustee, especially when you feel passionate about an issue. Admittedly, there have been times when I could have responded better than I did. As a school board member, please do your best to remember that your decisions affect children and their education. So do the work of regulating your emotions. The stronger you'll become mentally.

The Ego

So, let's talk about a delicate issue---the ego; also known as 'pride.' How does ego get in the way of becoming an excellent trustee? Your ego as a trustee impacts the board and staff, and if not held in check, could be detrimental to student learning. We are aware that ego and self-image are related, and that how you believe other people view you is a powerful factor in reactive behavior. Ego and emotion go hand in hand. If left unchecked, ego affects behavior negatively. Therefore, ego is seen from our perspective as one of the many factors that must be handled when exercising government.

People in positions of authority sometimes feel a sense of entitlement. There is frequently a sense of entitlement among those in positions of power and some degree of privilege. If not managed, ego-inclined people tend to push harder, talk louder, and demand more, which is a recipe for disaster if you're trying to devise a collaborative solution for the district.

We all have an ego. But it's how we deal with our egos that makes or breaks us trustworthy and valued school board members. When our ego gets the best of us and we react rather than act, the district loses, which means the children and families we were elected to serve also lose. The ego is a very smooth operator, often whispering in your ear, "It's okay, just let go and say what you need to say. You are entitled!" Some people have fallen for this devilish trick, including me.

A great metaphor is this: how many men are there in the ring during a boxing match? The correct answer is three. The two fighters and the referee. The best referees are there, but they have yet to be seen. The fighters are the stars.

The same is true for school districts. Believe it or not, school board members are not the stars. The students and district administrators are those who deserve the attention. We are there to guide, and that is all. Unfortunately, all too often, the headlines are filled with school board trustees' antics, which draw and take away the attention of those who truly deserve it.

At times, I tried my best just to let it go and walk away. If I'm being transparent, my ego left me alone with one agenda item but crawled back into the next one. One author stated, "But with time, you must realize that ego is something that will not die, and it will always be there in some form or another, hiding somewhere in your life." On his personal blog, Mehul Singla (2016) writes, "The ego is not your amigo. It will only disconnect you from others and in the end, will leave you alone and sad. Egoism is the anesthetic that dulls the pain of stupidity." My advice to trustees is that the first thing they have to do is control themselves.

The success story of the legendary Bobby Jones, a master at golf and founder of the greatest golf pageant, The Master's Tournament, is well-known in many circles. Before he became a golf master, he had to learn how to master himself and his ego. Jones was only five when he first swung a golf club, and by twelve he had beaten everyone at the local golf club.

However, Jones was also noted for his hot temper and soon picked up the nickname "Club Thrower" from those who knew him. Jones became good friends with Grandpa Bart, who helped out part-time in the Pro Shop. Bart, an excellent golfer in his day, retired from the game because of his arthritis, but working in the Pro Shop kept them in touch with the game he loved.

Bobby Jones entered the National Amateur Tournament at fourteen but came home a loser. "Bobby, you're good enough to win that tournament," Grandpa Bart told him. "But you never will until you can control your temper. You miss a shot, you get upset, you lose." Jones knew Grandpa Bart was right, but he was twenty-one years old before winning a tournament. Grandpa Bart smiled when Jones finally won, "Bobby was fourteen years old when he mastered the game of golf," Bart chuckled, "But he was twenty-one years old before he mastered himself." (Van Eken, p. 320)

Like the younger Bobby Jones, you will become part of the problem if you can't control yourself. Get your emotions under control. If they are not carefully kept, this cultivates a culture and an attitude where folks will think letting the ego dominate is what it takes to get to the top of the mountain. All of a sudden, your meetings will be about the egos of the trustees and not about the district's business, and meetings can become a huge, toxic waste of time.

For some when elected, we think that, by our station within the organization, we're supposed to be infallible, see-all, know-it-alls. Some trustees believe business will get done at the end of the day because *they* said so. One of the problems that many trustees find themselves in is that other members may have that same egoistic outlook. The book, *Discover Your True North,* (2015) makes the point that when many first assume the mantle of leadership, few leaders feel "completely ready." Stepping up to lead often moves us out of our comfort zones.

This is a natural response when facing any new challenge, mainly in which you are responsible for others. How you respond to this challenge determines whether or not you'll be experienced as authentic and trustworthy, or nervous and political. With ego comes a phenomenon known as imposter syndrome. This happens when folks find themselves taking on big roles without feeling like they are ready to do so. They compare themselves with established players and oftentimes get the feeling they shouldn't be there, because who are they? George continues in *True North* (2015) that many who have acquired power suffer from imposter syndrome and are uncomfortable and uncertain about how to use it. They are beset with doubts about shouldering the responsibilities of leadership. They know nothing! They're lying to themselves if they think they are competent.

How you manage your ego will determine how successful you are at becoming a great and long-serving trustee. I frequently hear stories about trustees who want to run into a boardroom, lay out all their goals, objectives, supporting information, and arguments on the table, and then say, "Here's what you should do." Then they get pushback from the other trustees, and they're trying to figure out where the dissonance is coming from. It's coming from the other trustees who feel disrespected because they are a governing *team*, not a one-trick pony. Good governance comes from understanding our emotions and others' perspectives.

The natural reaction to being challenged is a variation of the fight or flight response when you are listening, and you hear something contrary to how you perceive it. If you are not careful, you will cultivate a culture and attitude of using ego and its tricks to get to the top of the mountain. In the words of Epictetus, "It is impossible to learn that which one thinks one already knows. "When we let our ego tell us that we have arrived and figured it all out, it prevents us from learning." (Holiday, 2018) This can be difficult if one has a flimsy ego, especially when you have a different perspective.

Once there was a farmer who insulted his neighbor. Realizing his mistake, he went to the preacher to ask for forgiveness. The preacher told him to take a bag of feathers and drop them in the center of the town. The farmer did as he was told. Then the preacher asked him to go and collect the feathers and put them back in the bag. The farmer tried but couldn't, as the feathers had all blown away. When he returned with the empty bag, the preacher said, "The same thing is true about your words. You dropped them rather easily, but you can't retrieve them, so be very careful in choosing your words."

How will your ego and words affect the people around you once you become an elected official? We must remember that our seats do not belong to us but to the people who put us there. No matter how long your tenure, your role as a school board member is still temporary. We must remember that we are servants first and foremost, therefore, place that ego where it belongs. It's better to have a mission that makes sense and remember why you wanted to sit on the dais in the first place.

If you want to be an effective school board member, do the work of killing your pride before you lose your senses. You cannot let pride lead you astray. It would be best to remember that humility is the antidote to pride. Every day, remind yourself how much work remains to be done, not how much you have already completed.

The story is told that before Bill Belichick became the four-time Super Bowl-winning head coach of the New England Patriots, he made his way up the NFL's ranks by doing grunt work and making his superiors look good without getting any credit. When starting in our endeavors, we must make an effort to sacrifice short-term gratification for long-term gain. Learn from more seasoned board members, attend training, and learn to absorb everything you can. Forget credit.

Checking egos and staying humble without receiving credit is hard for most elected officials, but we must figure out how to let go of our controlling egos. The infectious need to control and micromanage everything is usually revealed in how one deals with success. Ego starts by saying, "It must all be done my way, even little things, even the inconsequential because that's how I have been succeeding so far."

Entitlement, Emotional Intelligence, and The Ego

Entitlement kills many political careers. An old method of catching wild turkeys can be an excellent lesson for all of us. To trap the turkeys, corn was scattered on the ground. Then a net was stretched about two feet high over the grain. When the wild turkeys sensed no human was near, they approached the corn and lowered their heads to eat it. Never lifting their heads, they would nibble the corn beneath the net. When they became full and tried to leave, instead of keeping their heads down, they raised their heads and were immediately caught in the net.

Could it be that when our heads are held too high, getting trapped by self-centeredness is inevitable? Could it be that we, like those turkeys, feel entitled to take what we want at whatever cost? The lesson: refuse the bait. Don't be a turkey.

Some view this position and title as a launching pad to higher offices. I get it. In many communities, school board races are competitive but don't get the press of the higher elected offices. If we are honest, many run for school board because they seek attention and prestige. These glory seekers are more concerned with their status and reputation than with building teams or organizations. When your motivations are primarily based on money, fame, power, and glory, you risk developing into a glory seeker over time, if you don't keep those motives in check.

Entitlement is one of the most harmful traits a school trustee can embody. We won the election, but that doesn't mean we can now run and push over the district's staff, teachers, and administrators. While parking in front of the school is nice, it doesn't mean you own it. We must remember that we are part of a governance *team* comprised of intelligent trustees who are all growing into their perceived roles. Reflective trustees regularly remind themselves of that fallibility and understand their limits yet strive to push those limits and grow. It's a simple concept but not easy to implement because of ... you guessed it ... our EGOS!

School board leaders with high emotional intelligence are better equipped to make decisions considering the impact on team members and stakeholders, as their sense of entitlement is *kept well in check*. They can weigh the potential consequences of their choices, understand the perspectives of others, and make decisions that align with the organization's goals and values. This results in more informed and thoughtful decisions that benefit the entire organization, not just individuals who feel they *deserve* whatever they're asking for.

Bridge Builder. Ambassador Between School and Community

Another significant benefit of emotional intelligence in leadership is that it fosters empathy. Leaders with high EI recognize and understand the emotions of others, which enables them to create a more inclusive work environment. They can connect with team members personally, build stronger relationships, and develop a sense of belonging that leads to increased engagement and productivity. Ron Sharon (2023) posted an article on LinkedIn, *The Unseen Powerhouse of Emotional Intelligence in Leadership,* which makes the case that leaders with strong emotional intelligence are better equipped to handle the pressures of the role, maintain a positive outlook, and inspire their team members to remain focused and motivated.

The most effective trustees are known for their empathy, enabling them to understand others' feelings even when no words are being spoken. This quality allows one to quickly create a plan of action to diffuse a situation by looking at it from others' perspectives, as well as one's own. Empathy also contributes to better leadership because it allows for validating all opinions, not just one person's. Empathy, combined with excellent communication skills, such as mediating conflicts, negotiating agreements, actively listening to others, and articulating essential ideas, are necessary for a good school board trustee.

The board is responsible for involving the community in appropriate, meaningful ways and communicating clear information to the community about district policies, educational programs, fiscal conditions, and progress on goals. Board members should speak up for the interests of the students they represent and are the only locally elected officials explicitly appointed to do so. Board members represent students, the district's educational initiatives, and public education. They build support within their communities and at the state and national levels.

Additionally, leaders with strong EI can more effectively communicate complex messages and provide constructive feedback that is received positively and encourages growth. One of the critical benefits of emotional intelligence (EI) in a leadership role is improved communication. Cynthia Kivland (2018) remarks in her article, *Successfully Managing Emotions and Behavior*, that leaders who possess a high degree of emotional intelligence are better able to understand the emotions of others and tailor their communication styles accordingly. This enables them to build stronger relationships with their team members, foster trust, and increase collaboration. (p. 68)

Trustees who build bridges between opposing sides of a dispute are known as 'bridge builders.' Regardless of profession, anyone can contribute to developing relationships across boundaries, cultures, religions, etc. Building bridges between opposing individuals and groups facilitates connections, enhances communication and fosters trust.

There will be instances where your district needs community support, whether it's to pass a bond, raise money to attend a field trip or put forth an issue that needs communicating. This is where you step in as a trustee and build the bridge between the community and this district. You may be asked to speak at, or attend, Kiwanis or Rotary meetings, conduct a radio interview, or invest time with a parent in the aisle of your local supermarket to provide the facts concerning a pressing issue.

Influential school board members work collaboratively with the community and staff. They also build a robust communication system to involve and inform internal and external stakeholders in creating and accomplishing district goals. School board members might give specific examples of how they engaged with and listened to the community in high-achieving districts.

Bridge building and emotional intelligence go hand in hand. Leaders who possess a high degree of EI are better able to understand the emotions of others and tailor their communication style accordingly. This enables them to build stronger relationships with their team members, foster trust, and increase collaboration. Additionally, leaders with strong EI can more effectively communicate difficult messages or provide constructive feedback that is received positively and encourages growth.

The Foye Factor: Hungry, Humble, And Smart

In the district I served, the previous superintendent had the executive cabinet read the best seller, *The Ideal Team Player: How to Recognize and Cultivate the Three Essential Virtues,* by Patrick Lencioni (2016). In his book, Lencioni describes the three virtues of team members: hungry, humble, and emotionally intelligent/smart (EI). Our district had an employee, Jeff Foye, who embodied these characteristics, so when he passed, the district coined these three virtues as The Foye Factor.

As a school board trustee, being hungry, humble, and smart is necessary for the role. It is said of Charles Dickens that people who met him for the first time often would never have suspected that he was the most distinguished literary man of his time. He never spoke of himself; he always took the most modest interest in the affairs of others, and they learned with surprise that the man who had just been talking with them so simply, showing such an interest in their affairs---was the literary star of his time.

In most corporate cultures, it's common for people with just one of the three qualities to last for a while on the team. However, individuals with two of the three can exist but may wreak havoc on the board by not seeing the big picture. I believe it takes all three attributes of being hungry, humble, and smart as an individual. When we view our role as school board members through this particular lens, we learn interesting things about those who might join our board, those who are already there, and even ourselves.

An excellent school board member is forward-thinking and has flexible ideas. They are innovative, open-minded individuals who constantly attempt to think outside the box to accomplish the desired outcome. They are proud of their creative and critical thinking abilities. Since they know the younger generation is the future, they also try to enlist more of them in their cause.

Being knowledgeable is only one aspect of school leadership. Trustees must be emotionally, socially, and psychologically intelligent to mobilize their community behind their causes. Trustees are individuals capable of handling difficult circumstances by using their intelligence and tempering it with humility, and a hunger to do more.

At this point, one must ask, "What happens when school board members have little to no emotional intelligence?" The following section deals with the consequences of failing to put student needs first in favor of promoting individual agendas.

Failure To Put Student Needs First

There are several ways that trustees fail to put student needs first. They engage in partisan politics, do not represent the district's interests, ignore the needs of marginalized communities, and/or engage in bullying and harassment, which all affect the overall classroom environment.

"Children may only represent 20-30 percent of our population, but they represent 100% of our future," said serial entrepreneur, Richard Branson. (2011) With this in mind, school board members are elected officials but are also expected to place children first because those children come from all walks of life and political affiliations.

Many school districts serve a diverse population, and school board members must recognize and address the unique needs of all students in the district. When board members ignore the needs of marginalized communities, such as English language learners, students with disabilities, or low-income students, it can perpetuate existing inequalities in the education system, and lead to a lack of progress toward creating a more equitable system.

Ineffective school board members put school improvement and student interests last. Instead, they utilize their position on the school board to advance a personal agenda. The most recent cultural sound bite is not something a seasoned trustee will listen to or let influence them. The best school board member places the students' needs first and meets them where they are. Personal agendas are when board members prioritize their personal agendas over the district's and its students' needs. These agendas can manifest in various ways, such as board members pushing for policies that benefit their interests or affiliations, rather than the broader community.

This behavior can lead to a lack of cooperation and collaboration among board members and prevent the board from making decisions that benefit all students in the district. As a seasoned school board member, I have witnessed first-hand the harmful effects of horrible school board member behavior against students, teachers, and the education system. When some board members exhibit unprofessional and disrespectful behavior, it can create a toxic environment that undermines the very purpose of the education system.

One example of atrocious school board behavior is when board members engage in bullying and harassment toward fellow board members, teachers, and administrators. This behavior can create a toxic work environment and make it difficult for individuals to feel safe and supported in their positions. This behavior can lead to legal action or disciplinary measures against the offending board members.

One particularly egregious example of horrible school board member behavior occurred in the Hamilton Township School District in New Jersey. In 2018, a group of school board members were caught on tape making racist and sexist comments about a fellow board member. The comments were so offensive that New Jersey Governor Phil Murphy called for the board member's resignation. This incident highlights the damaging effects of unprofessional and discriminatory school board member behavior. Such behavior can create a hostile and unwelcoming environment for students and teachers who belong to marginalized groups, further exacerbating existing inequalities in the education system, and becoming a wasted and inefficient use of taxpayer dollars.

Horrible school board member behavior can significantly impact the education system's finances. When board members engage in petty arguments and refuse to work together, it can lead to inefficient decision-making and wasted resources. (*Great Schools*, 2009) This, in turn, can lead to a decline in the quality of education and higher costs for the district. Board members must collaborate to make informed decisions that benefit the entire community.

Another significant effect of horrible school board member behavior is the impact on teacher morale. Teachers are essential to the education system and must feel supported and valued by their school board members. A significant effect of horrible school board member behavior affecting teacher morale is its impact on their ability to provide quality education to students. Teachers are the backbone of any education system. They must feel supported and respected by their school board members.

When school board members engage in disruptive behavior or fail to support teachers, it can create a hostile environment for teachers to work in. It presents a ripple effect on student achievement and the overall quality of education in the district which can lead to 'teacher burnout,' and ultimately lead to higher teacher turnover rates, increased human resources costs, and a decreased quality of education. Horrible school board member behavior can have far-reaching and devastating effects on the education system, students, and teachers. It can also damage the community's trust in the education system.

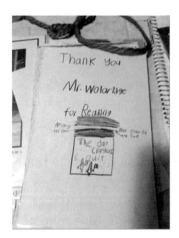

I love reading to students. The way they express their thanks is truly remarkable

Board members must always ask themselves the question, "What are we cultivating?" One of the books considered a true classic today is entitled, *As a Man Thinketh* by James Allen. (1902) The book states a man's mind may be like a garden that may be intelligently cultivated or allowed to run wild, but whether cultivated or neglected, it must and will *bring forth*. Just as a gardener cultivates his plot, keeping it free from weeds and growing the flowers and fruits he requires, a man tends the garden of his mind, weeding out all wrong, useless, and impure thoughts. (p. 7)

The trustee must choose to cultivate behavior that yields the flowers and fruits of good governance and refrain from madness. It's important for board members to act with professionalism, integrity, and respect at all times, and to prioritize the needs of all students in the district. As a seasoned school board member, I know first-hand the harm that disrespectful and unprofessional behavior can cause. It's essential for board members to always act with professionalism, respect, and integrity. Board members must remember that they are public servants and have a duty to work in the best interests of their community and the students they serve.

A fable relevant to the above concept is told about a young lion and a cougar. Both thirsty, the animals arrived at their usual water hole at the same time. They immediately began to argue about who should satisfy their thirst first. The argument became heated and each decided he would rather die than give up the privilege of being first to quench his thirst. As they stubbornly confronted each other, their emotions turned to rage. Their cruel attacks on each other were suddenly interrupted. They both looked up. Circling overhead was a flock of vultures, waiting for the loser to fall. Quietly, the two beasts turned and walked away. The thought of being devoured was all they needed to end their quarrel.

As servants act with professionalism, respect, and integrity at all times. When school board members fail to live up to these expectations, they do a disservice to their community and the future of the children they are supposed to serve. When we insist on quenching their own thirst before attending to the thirst of schools the vultures will begin to circle. But I pray the good trustees will remember what they are there for and let their students have their rightful place at the 'educational watering hole.'

School board members must remember that they are public servants tasked with ensuring students receive the best education possible. Immature trustee behavior can have far-reaching and devastating effects on the education system, students, and teachers. As a seasoned school board member, I urge those who want to serve to act professionally and respectfully. We must put aside personal agendas and work collaboratively to make informed decisions that benefit all students and teachers. By doing so, we can ensure that our education system provides the best possible education for our children to prepare them for a successful future.

I really enjoy serving.

Reflective Questions - Chapter 4

1. How can school board members develop and enhance their emotional intelligence to navigate the complexities of boardroom dynamics and foster positive relationships within the educational environment?

2. In what ways does the presence or absence of emotional intelligence impact the effectiveness of school board members in managing conflicts, facilitating constructive conversations, and making informed decisions for the benefit of the district?

3. How can trustees balance the need for assertiveness and leadership with the potential negative effects of ego, entitlement, and a lack of humility in their roles, especially when faced with challenging situations or conflicts within the school board?

Chapter 5

From Candidate to Contributor. Now What?

The First 100 Days

Campbell and Fullan's (2019) *The Governance Code,* Chapter 4, outlines what the current board and new trustees should do to welcome a new trustee. I highly recommend reading this text within the first 100 days of becoming a trustee. Now that you have been appointed or won the election, here are some best practices, tips, and general guidelines.

It's puzzling how any new trustee could be expected to be at the peak of their performance immediately after joining a board. In almost every organization, public and private, more attention is being given to the onboarding process. The board can take steps to help new trustees feel welcome. Current board members should make contact to introduce themselves, maybe invite the new member out for coffee or lunch.

This is accomplished by providing new employees with a full complement of tools, an explanation of the culture of the organization, and a clear definition of rules and responsibilities. There is a saying in government circles that one new trustee creates an entirely new board. And in many ways, how newly elected trustees are brought on to the governor's team determines how that board will function from that point on. I can't emphasize enough the importance of onboarding a new team member to the team---yet few organizations do it well.

I am thinking back about my first hundred days as a new trustee. After going through an interview process with the existing board members, they made me feel welcome and part of the team. While I do not recall formal sit-down conversations, I remember various tidbits about how the board works. Bruce, through his actions, showed me how to follow instructions. Cathy showed me how money works. Linda was a strategic thinker, and Cheryl was the member who stirred the drink. I can still see her sitting at the back of the boardroom and at the head of the table, facing us all and directing traffic. While she was a woman of few words during closed and open sessions, I could tell that she had a command of the room and the office.

Throughout my tenure, I had to learn by observation. While I may have had ideas, I had yet to earn the right to move forward. Here is where emotional intelligence once again surfaces as an important part of a trustee's tenure. Emotional intelligence is vital, especially during your first 100 days. But it doesn't stop there. I advise any new member to take a year or two to learn the process and people because it will take that much time to truly be in sync with your new team.

Onboarding is a three-way street between the new member(s), the existing members, and the superintendent. Each person has a responsibility to one another in this process. When one new member takes the oath of office, the board is now a new entity. "Every time a new trustee joins the board, it's a new board," (Campbell & Fullan, 2019, p. 77). Campbell and Fullan suggest four mindset shifts for existing members and the superintendent when onboarding new members:

1. Begin afresh with system-wide coherence and the district's moral imperative.
2. Introduce the new trustee to the board's governance culture.
3. Orient the new trustee regarding the concept of a governance mindset.
4. Reinforce the focus of the existing members to introduce the new members and make them a welcome member of the governance team.

When I was first appointed, Kip took the opportunity to walk me around the schools and meet the principals and teachers of the district that I would be serving. It was eye-opening for me to see how schools operated behind the scenes, which influenced my future decision-making. In addition, during our drives between campuses and conferences, we got to know each other better and solidified the concept of governing as a team.

New Trustee - First 100 Days (Manage your Expectations)

I get that you made promises and want to make a great impression on your new colleagues and those who voted for you. Many of us have been told that the first impression is the most important one. Please be patient if you were elected for a term of office and take advantage of the time to learn.

Unfortunately, I have heard horror stories where onboarding a new trustee went horribly wrong, which caused havoc for the board and the district. While this list is not exhaustive, here are my five tips for new trustees in their first hundred days.

Learn and Observe

Take the time to learn and observe the district's culture, processes, and dynamics. It's in everyone's best interest and makes the most sense to understand how things function and be attentive to the expectations and standards inside the district. Invest the time and effort to learn about governance. Many new trustees have confessed that being on the board was an entirely unexpected experience, no matter how many board meetings they attended or conversations they had with people they believed they knew. I remember my first few meetings as a novice board member --and wow! Nothing prepared me for the speed, scope, and complexity of those meetings!

When it came to the press and propaganda, I quickly realized that the media and people I talked to meant well, but they only possessed half of the picture. While they may have meant well, I quickly reduced commentary and focused on the facts. Many times, when it comes to school issues half the picture is many times worse than none of the picture.

One Mouth, Two Ears

I don't doubt that you already possess excellent communication skills. You can articulate your thoughts precisely and have insightful analysis and strong opinions. But remember to listen attentively to others as well. Those trustees before you have insight and history you don't possess. You will also quickly find out that the educational system uses a different language, and you will need to become fluent in that language, to function effectively at your new job.

Within the first one hundred days of taking the oath, make sure you ask questions, seek explanations when necessary, and keep others informed about your progress and the difficulties you face. Commit yourself to intensive learning, as you cannot participate in something you don't fully comprehend. (Campbell & Fullan, 2019, p. 41)

In addition, be careful when you say you researched a topic. Many school board members, including some individuals, have earned their Ph.D. or Ed.D. With these folks, mentioning your research brings up another connotation, and if a strong relationship needs to be built, one with research experience may challenge you on your research methodology and framework. This is an excellent way of saying that if you Googled it and drew a conclusion, you didn't research it, and depending on your relationship with your new colleagues, they may call you out on it.

Seek Out a Mentor

Dedicate some of your time to determining whether members of the board or the district can act as mentors for you. This advice saved me from experiencing a great deal of emotional distress and physical anguish when I was first appointed, and even today I continue to consult with and seek advice from current, and former board members and superintendents.

Even though many board members join the board with ideas and goals related to a specific agenda or area of special interest, new trustees discover that it is challenging, if not impossible, to carry out a systemic oversight responsibility if they have only one goal or conviction. Although trustees' passion and beliefs must propel them, it's important to avoid going too far because of the dangers this poses. Reach out to other trustees who have previously served on this board and ask for their advice and direction. Leverage the knowledge and expertise of these individuals to navigate problems and speed up your learning curve.

Maintain a High Level of Professionalism

How can I put this delicately? When you first start serving on a board of trustees, you have no idea about the things you'll encounter that you don't know. Do your best to keep your overzealousness under control, even if your personality is like a bull in a china shop. Let go of whatever preconceived views you may have regarding the proper operation of school boards.

Keep in mind that you are now a member of a team. Yes, you were elected as an individual but must govern as a team member. You did not get to pick the team, and you may not even like everyone on the team---but it is your team!

Understand that no one trustee has the authority as an individual trustee to fix the problems you promised to fix in your campaign; only the board has the authority to take action. The general public very rightly tends to judge the board's performance based on its accomplishments, rather than the actions of specific people. A 'lone ranger' attitude benefits no one and is harmful to all.

Ask For Feedback

Ask for feedback regularly, both from your fellow trustees and the superintendent. While no one person is in charge of the other, it's wise to seek feedback to improve. It's okay to solicit both critical feedback and ideas. This demonstrates your commitment to improvement but also assists you in efficiently adapting to the new environment. I currently am serving with a newly elected trustee, and is constantly asking me ... "Is this, okay?" ..." Did I say that right?" ... "Can I ask this question?" The answer to each of these questions is yes. I appreciate the willingness to learn and ask for feedback on how she is viewed by her colleagues, district staff, and stakeholders.

The moves a new trustee makes in their first hundred days, and I would add the first cycle are critical. It goes without saying that it's of the utmost importance to be punctual, reliable, and respectful to both your fellow members and the district staff. Here is a tip: current members are paying close attention to whether or not they can trust you. They are particularly concerned about whether or not you will keep confidentiality and ethical standards.

Your attitude, body language, and demeanor set the tone of how your fellow trustees will embrace you, or not. I have heard hundreds of stories where a new school board member misstepped, and the older trustees held it against them for years. Yes, this may be immature, but it happens. As some new trustees have indicated, the goal is not to indoctrinate or brainwash you. It's about the team. Team first! Governance first! Remember, you are there to serve the children, not the loudest voice in your head.

Where Does My Loyalty Lie?

When I am coaching sitting school board members, the overarching dilemma I constantly revisit is how to balance the needs of those who voted for us---versus the needs of the district when these needs conflict. I will admit that this is a tricky situation that I wrestle with even today.

In the article *Winning the Election is Only Half the Battle: A Guide to Governing*, Neil Reiff (2016) provides a comprehensive guide for newly elected officials on how to govern effectively after winning an election. In many cases, Reiff emphasizes that while winning the election is a significant achievement, governing effectively is an entirely different challenge.

Officials have wrestled with this challenge which is now at the forefront, as many face the scrutiny and limelight of election.

Unlike city council, supervisor, state, and national elected officials who have insights into building a solid team, establishing priorities, and navigating the political landscape, many school board members face this alone and without experience.

Believing that politics will not enter school boards makes for a naïve trustee. You ran on change. You promised those who voted for you that you would "shake things up" with no rubber stamping on your watch. It was those sentiments and conversations that got you elected. However, once you take the oath of office, you may realize that what was promised may not be reality. In the seminal book on school board governance, Campbell and Fullan compare politics and governance:

Politics Without Good Governance

- Peaks before, during, and just after elections
- Caters to special interest groups
- Often superficial, bumper sticker style
- Can be sincere but weak in implementation
- Harmful when lacking good governance
- Limited last benefit
- Politics with Good Governance
- Builds capacity relative to core agenda
- Recognizes that government is for all the people
- Long-term as well as short-term perspective
- Implementation versus adoption mindset (p. 5)

There is a resurgence or emerging sentiment many Americans are feeling under in our national politics. While our country has differences, ideological gaps are widening resulting in greater polarization. As a result, school boards have again become the place for a renewed focus on local politics, where everyday people can directly impact their communities and their role in them.

Schools are foundational to any society and are flashpoints of discussion if not careful division. Many school districts in California have transitioned from at-large elections to local trustee areas. So, the question becomes, "Am I loyal to the residents of my trustee area that elected me, or the students in the school district?" I agree with Campbell and Fullan who make the point that this is a false dichotomy, and many ask the wrong question. "Trustees cannot allow themselves to be forced into an artificial choice: trustee area versus the district---a few children versus all children." The authors go on to remind a newly elected trustee that a commitment to a proper governance mindset leads to systems and strategic thinking which places equity and quality instruction for all children. (p.100)

I believe in the importance of listening to constituents and responding to concerns. But it's also important to remember that even those who elected you have agendas that may be wrong for the students in the district. Many community members, especially those in lower economic and minority communities, are intimated by the board room, so they are unwilling to appear before you. But the price of their silence is that they are often most affected by unethical policies and practices. As their trustees, we are responsible for ensuring their voices are heard and their needs are addressed.

Admittedly, there are tremendous pressures and challenges facing newly elected trustees. Nick Corasaniti's 2016 New York Times article, *You Won the Election. Now What?* explores the challenges that newly elected officials face as they transition from campaigning to governing, making the point that officials should prioritize issues important to their constituents and be prepared to make tough decisions and tradeoffs to achieve their goals. Our obligation as school board members is to look after all our students, not just those whose parents are loud and organized. Good trustees prioritize the voices and needs of marginalized communities and underrepresented groups.

In 2009, I participated in Kern Leader's Academy for upcoming business leaders. My mentor, Michael Turnipseed, the program's founder and director brought together the best in our community to share their insights and thoughts on governance with my classmates and me. We had two readings: Saul Alinsky's 1989 *Rules for Radicals,* and *A Profile in Courage* by John F. Kennedy (1955). Kennedy's book discusses the concept of political courage. It examines various instances where these elected officials made principled decisions, even when they went against popular opinion or posed career risks. This text still has a profound impact on me.

There are three incidents that Kennedy recounts that amaze me. The first is the story of Daniel Webster as an exemplar of political courage. Daniel Webster, a prominent senator from Massachusetts in the 19th century, is recognized for his unwavering commitment to preserving the Union and the principles of the Constitution.

There was a moment in Webster's career when he delivered a speech in support of the Compromise of 1850, which included controversial provisions such as the Fugitive Slave Act. The Fugitive Slave Act mandated the return of escaped, enslaved people to their owners, even from free states, causing deep moral conflicts and widespread opposition among abolitionists.

Kennedy recounts that despite Webster's opposition to slavery, he believed preserving the Union and maintaining peace was crucial for the nation's stability. He saw the Compromise of 1850 as a way to prevent the Union's dissolution and preserve the delicate balance between free and enslaved states. Webster's decision to endorse the Compromise of 1850 and uphold the Fugitive Slave Act went against many in his home state of Massachusetts, where anti-slavery sentiments ran deep. His support for the compromise drew significant criticism and caused a rift within his party. Kennedy portrays Webster's stand as political courage, highlighting his willingness to put aside personal beliefs and face the backlash to preserve the Union. Despite his criticism, Webster remained steadfast in his conviction that compromise was necessary to maintain national unity.

Next, is the remarkable story of John Quincy Adams, the sixth President of the United States, who stands as an example of political courage and integrity. Here, Kennedy focused on Adams' post-presidential career as a congressman, where he consistently stood up against the institution of slavery, despite the prevailing sentiments and interests of his constituents. Adams firmly believed in the immorality of slavery and was determined to fight for its abolition. It's well known that in an age of slavery and its accepted practice, Adams didn't even own slaves. He instead hired white laborers when needed. He was a man ahead of his times, and courageous to stand up to the institution of slavery in the face of strong, opposing forces.

Adams' most notable act of courage came in the case of the Amistad, a ship carrying African captives who had rebelled against their captors. As a member of Congress, Adams took on the legal defense of the Amistad captives before the Supreme Court. Despite facing tremendous pressure to abandon the case and the risk of alienating his constituents, Adams fearlessly advocated for the rights of the Africans and argued for their freedom. Through his brilliant legal arguments, Adams convinced the Supreme

Court to rule in favor of the Amistad captives, securing their freedom and affirming that all individuals have inherent rights, regardless of race or origin.

My favorite of the three stories is Sam Houston's. It's highlighted as an exemplary display of political courage and integrity. Despite being a strong advocate for states' rights and the independence of Texas, Houston believed that secession was not in the nation's best interest and would only lead to further division and conflict. When the issue of secession arose, Houston, as the governor of Texas at the time, refused to endorse the state's move toward secession.

Houston's opposition to secession put him at odds with many of his constituents who favored leaving the Union. Houston firmly stood by his convictions despite the intense pressure and threats to his political career. He delivered a passionate speech to the Texas legislature, urging them to reconsider their decision and warning of the dire consequences of secession. However, his efforts were unsuccessful, and Texas seceded from the Union in March of 1861. Kennedy portrays Houston as a principled leader who made a courageous stand for what he believed was in the nation's best interest.

These three examples showcase political courage. Their stories remind us that authentic leadership sometimes requires going against popular opinion and standing up for one's convictions, even in the face of adversity. Many of us who pay attention to both business and politics are aware of the ethical challenges that public officials face in balancing the demands of their constituents with their moral principles.

As a business professor at my local community college, I have stated to my students that those in positions of power must be careful and diligent to guard their morality. In the last few years, I have seen that there is so much pressure on elected officials to cater to their constituents' interests that it often compromises ethical and moral standards.

I believe that those individuals who prioritize the demands of only their constituents may end up supporting policies that harm marginalized communities or perpetuate systemic injustices. I believe that as a school board member, it's in the district's best interest to serve the students' interests, rather than just their most vocal constituents, and I practice this concept religiously. If it costs me re-election---it is what it is. You're probably asking yourself, "If I don't advocate for those who elected me, am I not being faithful and true to my constituents?" Many trustees felt this way at one time or another, and it's a real and valid question that needs answering.

Unfortunately, the statesman is a foreign or antediluvian idea in our current political climate. This is why you should avoid overcommitting or making promises you cannot keep while campaigning. I advise school board members to prioritize issues important to the district, then stakeholders, and be willing to make tradeoffs where necessary.

If you remember that you have only one vote---you are one voice that is part of a governing body, which makes it easier. By all means, advocate! Speak up! Challenge the status quo. Honest and open debate are vital to the democratic process. There is nothing wrong with this. But **how** you do it becomes the issue. Will you pout? Sulk? Contact the media and hold your press conference. I'm reiterating that you are a member of a governance team, and if the vote doesn't go your way, how you handle this situation will either hurt or help your governance team.

It Is a Tightrope

Now, is what I've written here telling you to go against your personal beliefs and ethics? No! School board members should not sacrifice personal integrity and ethics to satisfy their constituents. This is where a commitment to wisdom is crucial to effective governance and must lead the way.

As a trustee, you may face the dilemma of choosing between meeting the demands of your constituents and adhering to your personal principles, which may be at odds with popular opinion. This can cause conflict because school board members are expected to be representatives of their constituents and obey the law. This creates tension between their duty to represent their constituents' interests and acting in the best interests of the students. I live in a very tight-knit community and struggle with the fact that it's difficult for school board members to balance their personal convictions with those of various interest groups. I can't tell you how many instances I faced pressure from family, friends, and those who hold higher political offices than mine, to prioritize the needs of specific groups over others.

When faced with this issue, I do my best to remind them that as a school board member, I must represent the interests of all my stakeholders, regardless of their community stature, political influence, or lack thereof. This stance takes courage and has lost me a few friends. But I believe that in this current political climate, if we are not careful in this nonpartisan seat, the influence of a few can lead to policies that serve the interests of the few rather than the many.

I will admit it. This is hard work. My family will tell you how many times they've heard me mumbling to myself or asking them questions on how to resolve this conflict while wrestling between two opinions. School board members engage in a process of ethical reflection that involves considering the values and principles that underlie our decisions. During the pandemic, I engaged with a friend and ethics professor at California State University, Bakersfield, to ensure that my thought process and votes were based on sound ethical principles while considering the views and needs of all relevant parties, not just my favorite news outlet, opinion pages, and country club chatter.

Max Steir, CEO of the Partnership for Public Service, a nonpartisan, nonprofit organization dedicated to improving the federal government's effectiveness, wrote a 2020 article in the Harvard Business Journal, *A Nonpartisan Model for Developing Public-Service Leaders.* (2020) Stier proposed a novel approach to developing public-service leaders. Rightly so, Stier argues that the current political climate has made it difficult for public service leaders to navigate the complex landscape of government, where polarizing ideologies and political pressure can interfere with effective leadership. He proposes a nonpartisan model enabling leaders to focus on their job responsibilities and providing a framework for effective collaboration across party lines based on three fundamental principles: leadership development, collaboration, and innovation. I agree with Steir's formulation. As a veteran trustee, I find this model provides a compelling argument for effective school board governance that will survive in a complex, political landscape.

As discussed earlier, this model is not without its challenges, particularly in an increasingly polarized political climate. However, it provides a framework for developing leaders to navigate the complexities of government to work collaboratively across party lines, ethically and responsively, and strives to meet the needs of all members of their constituents.

Working collaboratively is key. Comprise isn't a dirty word. The 18th-century economist, philosopher, and educator, Edmund Burke, reminds those who have the honor of being elected trustees with this sage advice: "That every human benefit, every virtue and every prudent act is founded on compromise."

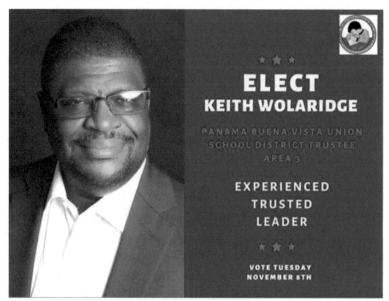

Campaign Slogan 2022

Reflective Questions - Chapter 5

1. How can a school board ensure a smooth onboarding process for new trustees, considering the importance of the first 100 days and the impact on the board's overall effectiveness?

2. In what ways does emotional intelligence play a crucial role during the initial phase of a trustee's tenure, and how can existing board members and the superintendent contribute to fostering a positive and collaborative atmosphere?

3. How does the balance between representing the interests of those who elected a trustee and the broader responsibility to the entire school district manifest, and what strategies can trustees employ to navigate this complex dynamic effectively?

Epilogue

My Mask

We Wear the Mask
Paul Laurence Dunbar, 1872 –1906

We wear the mask that grins and lies;
It hides our cheeks and shades our eyes,
This debt we pay to human guile;
With torn and bleeding hearts we smile
And a mouth with myriad subtleties,
Why should the world be over-wise,
In counting all our tears and sighs?
Nay, let them only see us, while
We wear the mask.
We smile, but oh great Christ, our cries
To thee from tortured souls arise;
We sing, but oh the clay is vile
Beneath our feet, and long the mile,
But let the world dream otherwise,
We wear the mask!

I don't know any elected official, especially a Black elected official, who doesn't understand this poem. This section is hard to contemplate, let alone write. The mask is heavy. What many do not recognize is the discomfort of wearing it. We have worn it so much that we forget it's there.

It was a glorious night. I was appointed to my District's school board. It was a monumental moment because I was the first African American ever appointed to serve on my board of trustees since the school district's inception, which spans over 125 years!

The night that the vote results were announced, my name was announced as the chosen one. I saw the pride in my late pastor, Dr. Sam Thomas, as he looked at me and we embraced. Honestly, I didn't think I had a shot and was elated by what happened. I was joyful! I shook the hands of those in the audience, including my competitors. I got in my car and went home, so happy to tell my wife and daughters. The next day, my wife and I took our daughters out of class and we went into Kip's office who was the superintendent, where I lifted my right hand and took the oath of office to protect and defend the Constitution of the United States, and the State of California. That evening, I called my parents and I could hear the pride in their voices. I remember my late father saying, "Well, I be! That's all right." While I could not see them, I could hear the tears in my mother's voice as she congratulated me.

After calling a few more close family members and friends, the joy of that time dissipated. I appreciate the honor that comes with being an elected official; what I underappreciated or misunderstood was that being a black elected official in my county comes with a tremendous amount of pressure, as I'm sure it does in most other counties across the nation. It's nice to stand up at many events, wave at the audience as they call my name, and receive the thrill of applause. What I didn't realize and underestimated the pressure of being the first in this office. How does one survive? I look back 14 years later and realize I wore, and still wear, a mask. Except for my family and dear friends, people no longer saw Keith Wolaridge as the banker, a pretty good golfer, and a cool dude. Many looked past and didn't see the father. They don't see the husband. Many don't see board members as Oakland Raiders and Lakers fans; they see elected officials and in my case, they saw Keith Wolaridge as the first Black Panama Buena Vista Union School District representative. And for some, they probably saw a potential pawn to be used for their benefit.

Being the first comes with consequences. On more than one occasion, in the public square or board meetings, I bit my lip and stayed silent and smiled after a voter or community leader told a racist joke or made an offensive statement. Essayist and novelist, James Baldwin, in his 1955 essay, *Stranger in the Village,* describes the reaction of "smiling" as being a great part of the American Negro's "education." When uncomfortable or uneasy, and maybe angry, to cope and survive---we smile. Baldwin wrote that "Smile and the world smiles with you routine works well in this situation, as it had in many situations for which it was designed, which is to say that it did not work at all." (p. 115) I smile because I must make people like me. I smile in public while fuming privately. Countless times, often had to hold my tongue. Sometimes I scratched when I didn't itch and danced to music with no swing.

When you are the only one who must understand what it means to be under the microscope, that your life is not your own, and that the slightest foible or flaw "can and may be used against you" so you sit back and take it on the chin. And it's exhausting!

Often when you are the first person of color that has matriculated up the ladder, it is an unwritten rule you keep your mouth shut and your hands in your pockets. I really experienced this during campaign season and in the midst of the Obama and Trump eras. Some of the stuff people said in front of me was overwhelming---but I stayed quiet. I've had discussions with many Black people who felt I must hold my tongue, watch what I say, or say it in a palatable and digestible tone so that others will, quote-unquote, "accept me." And for some Blacks believe that "they have arrived," which mutes their voices into silence. For too long, many of us have tailored our messages at the expense of change within our communities. (Gilliam, 2020)

I would suggest that many minorities, whether elected or not, if honest with themselves, they too have faced this dilemma. Dr. Eddie Glaude, Jr., (2021), Professor of Religion at Princeton University in a speech entitled, *Take Giant Steps for Your Full Self*, places the silence this way. "Oftentimes, we are socialized to quiet ourselves. Socialized as a condition for our entree to mute who we take ourselves to be. We quiet our voices so that people aren't uncomfortable around us. We accept what people say about who we are, and then we begin to believe that we lack capacity, that we lack talent, that we don't have what it takes to succeed or to flourish in the world." The great poet and novelist, Maya Angelou, describes it as, "The traditional ruse to shield Black vulnerability, laughing to keep from crying."

The Harvard-trained and great sociologist, W. E. B. Dubois (1902) in his work, *The Souls of Black Folks,* labeled this phenomenon as 'double consciousness'. He states that double consciousness is:

"A peculiar sensation, this sense of always looking at oneself through the eyes of others, of measuring one's soul by the tape of a world that looks on in amused contempt and pity. One ever feels his two-ness—an American, a Negro; two souls, two thoughts, two unreconciled strivings; two warring ideals in one dark body, whose dogged strength alone keeps it from being torn asunder. The history of the American Negro is the history of this strife—-this longing to attain self-conscious manhood, to merge his double self into a better and truer self. In this merging, he wishes neither of the older selves to be lost. Such a double life, with double thoughts, double duties, and double, social classes, must give rise to double words and double ideas, and tempt the mind to pretense or revolt, to hypocrisy or radicalism." (p.77)

This is where the addictive and enslaving 'drug of acceptance' comes into play. Wearing the moniker of being "the first" many times means within the Black community that, *I'm not Black enough for mine,* and *too Black for theirs.* The fear of being ostracized by both sides becomes a snare, causing fatigue.

In the article, *What Are Black Fatigue and Code Switching and Why Do They Matter to Organizations?* by Patricia Sauceda Kramer and Kiana Atkins of the National Institute of Health, the writers identify and agree with author, organization consultant and strategist Mary-Frances Winter's definition of 'Black Fatigue' as, "Repeated variations of stress that result in extreme exhaustion and cause mental, physical and spiritual maladies that are passed down from generation to generation."

Even progressive workplaces must be aware of the issues that Black fatigue presents, to ensure an equitable and psychologically safe environment. (Kramer and Atkins, 2023) 'Code-switching' or adjusting one's normal behavior to fit into an environment, has long been a strategy for professional, Black individuals to navigate interracial interactions successfully. It often occurs in spaces where negative stereotypes of Black individuals run counter to what is considered appropriate or professional behaviors and norms in a specific environment, and it regularly happens in work settings. For many Black professionals, changing one's speech, look, conduct, or expression to make others more at ease in exchange for better treatment, more favorable service, or a better job, is an example of 'code-switching.'

Many Black people frequently resort to code-switching when they find themselves in situations where "appropriate" actions and standards run counter to the negative perceptions of Black people that are prevalent in that setting. Some examples of advice to Black people are:

- How to deal with police encounters
- Acting politely and respectfully when stopped
- Avoid running, even if you're afraid.

The article, *The Costs of Code Switching*, stresses that "While it is frequently seen as crucial for professional advancement, code-switching often comes at a great psychological cost. It has long been a method for black people to negotiate interracial encounters successfully, and these adjustments in behavior have significant ramifications for black people's well-being, economic growth, and even physical survival." (McCluney, Robotham, Lee, Durkee; 2019)

I remember one meeting discussing the need for more progress for our African American students in the district. Being an African American, I am highly concerned about that particular demographic, but I felt my District was slow-rolling the issue. I brought it up and I could sense the tension in the room.

One member asked me, "Do you have an agenda?"

I responded, "I don't have an agenda, but I do care about the achievement gap that these African American students, especially these boys, are so far behind."

That encounter told me right then and there that there are some topics that this district does not want to address, and I will admit that I stayed silent about them. I don't believe at that time we had the intestinal fortitude to move this work forward in an intentional manner. This is not a criticism of my fellow trustees, because when you deal with the issues of Black and white in this country, the issue can quickly become inflammatory. But we must understand that we serve to help students first, and we sometimes forget that. Plus, I let it go because I didn't have the votes or cache to move forward on it, so I didn't push the issue.

Another reason I stayed quiet was because of the 'fear of backlash' because the fear of antagonism and retribution has an extremely tight grip. While I'm an elected official of color, I still possess an unspoken fear of blowback, because history has a way of repeating itself. Backlash in the 21st century is not about visible violence; rather it works its way through the courts, the legislatures, and a range of government bureaucracies. It doesn't wear sheets, burn crosses, or take to the street, it works the halls of power, and it can achieve its ends far more effectively, and far more destructively. (Anderson, 2017). All one has to do is look at the Florida and Texas State legislatures to validate this point.

For almost 11 years, I stayed quiet when in a closed session I just could not take it anymore. That's when I lashed out. I was pissed off at what I perceived as the lack of intentionality in ensuring that our African American, male students got the attention they deserved to get the best education we could provide.

At that moment, I could only think about James Baldwin's phrase in the documentary film, *The Price of the Ticket*. Baldwin says,

"You always told me it takes time. It has taken my father's time, my mother's time, my uncle's time, my brothers' and sisters' time, and my nieces' and nephews' time. How much time do you want for your 'progress'?" (Kauffman, 2020)

Black people are proud to have a seat at the table; the price of the ticket has been paid by our ancestors. But we must recognize that this coveted seat must be more than just decorative and ornamental. I'm sad to report that some Black folks reside at this table just to add a line to their resume. Some folks of color reside in the chair and become peacocks for self-admiration and self-aggrandizement. They would never dare do anything that may get them 'excused' from the table. Sadly, many refuse to risk making life better for those behind them and will giggle and smile just to stay seated. To

When I think of this, my mind immediately refers to when Dr. Eddie Glaude (2016), in his groundbreaking book, *Democracy in Black,* refers to the sociologist E. Franklin Frazier's description of some Black folk' that sit at the table as "exaggerated Americans" who were willing to forget the wounds of the past and conform to the demands of white people in the most minute of details. (p. 231) Their presence at the proverbial table must be substantial if change and difference are to occur.

Dr. King was critical of this population as well. He scolded the middle, upper-middle, and upper-class Blacks for their complacency in his 1963 famous essay, *Letter From A Birmingham Jail*, Dr. King made the point that these are those who, as a result of long years of oppression, are so drained of self-respect and a sense of "somebodies" that they've adjusted, because of their academic and economic security, and have become insensitive to the problems of the masses and profit. (Edwards, 2018, p. 143) echo this sentiment, Thomas N. Todd is known for saying, "Some would rather switch than fight."

There was one instance where, after a breakfast meeting with the superintendent, a voter, a grandparent, and, I believe, a person of good intentions approached me in the parking lot because he had heard that our district was teaching Critical Race Theory. He conveyed that he did not want his grandson to be told that "white people were evil and the cause of the world's problems."

After gathering myself, I asked the elderly gentleman where he had heard this.

He paused and said, "The news." I asked again, "What channel?" He said, "Fox."

I responded, "In what school in our district were we teaching CRT?"

He was silent. I waited. Then, he said, "I heard." I asked again, "From whom?"

No response. From there, I asked a few more probing questions.

"How many books have you read on the subject or watched any documentaries about the genesis of CRT? Where was it founded?" Silence.

After a moment, which seemed like a lifetime, he admitted he had not read or watched anything on the subject.

While I've read my fair share on this topic, wisdom took over. There was a slight pause, and because of his age and because I was raised not to lecture my elders, we shook hands in the parking lot and wished each other a pleasant day. It is my prayer that this voter believes that decisions are made in a way that considers the diverse needs and interests of all members of society.

As a school board member, I like to believe that I'm transparent and accountable for my responses. Because of the mask, it can be difficult to be true and open about your decision-making processes and willing to explain my reasoning to stakeholders. I believe my questions, and the elderly gentleman's ensuing silence spoke volumes.

Dunbar's poem, *We Wear The Mask*, acknowledges the fact that many African Americans feel they must put on a "mask" of cheerfulness to conceal their inner pain from "the world" (which we may here describe as "the white world"). I know many Black people I talk to about this and they frequently report feeling socially conditioned or coerced into acting as though everything is fine---despite inner turmoil. The pain is unique because it directly results from our race. I have grown accustomed to seeming unaffected by this and hiding my sadness. I, and many of us, prefer to put on this figurative mask, which contributes to the dream and fantasy the rest of the world has told itself until pretending becomes second nature.

If I could go back in time and do it again, what would I do differently? I've asked this existential question time and again. There are three things I believe I would do differently if I could:

Speak up. Yes, say something. It might be uncomfortable for a brief while, but my soul and voice matter too. There are times I'm tired of treading lightly and sweet-talking and want to tell folks about the hell we are catching in these streets.

Leave my silo. Looking back, I would reach out to others who are in my shoes and provide support to discuss the frustrations of wearing the mask. Understanding that I am not by myself, and neither are they.

Have the courage to live in my authenticity. I believe I can speak for many, if not most, that we who are darker than blue for the sake of survival and sustainability leave our true selves in the driveway of our homes, street curbs, and parking lots. As you have read this can wear on and erode the soul. Looking back, I believe that I could have resisted the urge to sequester myself and bring all of me to the table. In 2020 I authored the book *Five Pillars* and the virtue of courage is one of those evergreen pillars. Looking back, I believe I could have trusted God for the courage to speak truth to power and to politicians; bring a voice of common sense and dignity, not only to myself but to others as well.

Years ago, I wish I could find it now, I watched a vignette on YouTube where a professional African American man, in his mid-forties, wearing a suit and a tie, carrying a briefcase, is in an alley. While in the alley he approaches the dumpster, sets his briefcase on top of it and opens his case, then begins to dump items out of it. These items include his dashiki, next was a picture of Dr. King. He continues to pull and throw away the album, Greatest Hits of The Temptations; and lastly, he holds his afro pick and tosses it into the can. While doing this his younger self is watching. He is begging, pleading, yelling, screaming please don't do this. Finally, in a fit of rage, the professional black man picks up his younger self, throws him into the dumpster, and slams it shut.

After gathering himself, he closes his briefcase, and begins to walk away, only to hear the can open and his younger self peaks his head out and says, "You forgot your pick".

114

The mask is one of the most pressing problems African Americans face in the workplace and the boardroom. Switching rather than fighting and hiding behind the mask may be essential to getting ahead in your professional or political career. Still, it often comes with a high, emotional cost and, Lord knows, I've got the receipts.

I end where I began in this chapter:

We wear the mask that grins and lies;
It hides our cheeks and shades our eyes,
This debt we pay to human guile;
With torn and bleeding hearts we smile
And a mouth with myriad subtleties,
Why should the world be over-wise,
In counting all our tears and sighs?
Nay, let them only see us, while
We wear the mask.
We smile, but oh great Christ,
our cries To thee from tortured souls arise.
We sing, but oh the clay is vile
Beneath our feet, and long the mile,
But let the world dream otherwise.
But let the world dream otherwise,
We wear the mask!

Special Thanks To.....

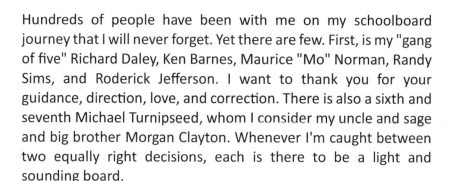

Hundreds of people have been with me on my schoolboard journey that I will never forget. Yet there are few. First, is my "gang of five" Richard Daley, Ken Barnes, Maurice "Mo" Norman, Randy Sims, and Roderick Jefferson. I want to thank you for your guidance, direction, love, and correction. There is also a sixth and seventh Michael Turnipseed, whom I consider my uncle and sage and big brother Morgan Clayton. Whenever I'm caught between two equally right decisions, each is there to be a light and sounding board.

Next are my pillars: my beautiful and understanding wife, Joanne, and our four, accomplished, intelligent, and gorgeous daughters: Christianna, Caylyn, Cheyenne, and Courtney. Many will never understand the stress and strain you endured while I was on the school board. You also served; not by casting a hard vote, but by being the spouse and children of an elected official. Girls it must have been demanding and stressful. Every day you went to school under the microscope and scrutiny. I'm sure the implied expectations were different, and you handled the pressure with grace and dignity. For this, Daddy, thank you!

I'd also like to thank the two ladies who keep me organized as a board member. The best executive assistants are Patty Patterson and Sandi Taylor. I would lose the nose on my face were it not been for you. And a 'special thank you' for ensuring my hotel rooms were always below the 10th floor.

Next, are my superintendents, the three K's: Kip, Kevin, and Katie. Each of you made me a better trustee. Your patience, wisdom, direction, and friendship will never be forgotten. Kip, you inherited the budget devastation of 2009–2010. Kevin, new laws were passed that challenged you professionally and personally; and Katie, your first year was the pandemic. The general public has no idea of the stress and strain of your job, and each of you held your head high and led the district higher during these challenges. Even when we disagreed, you heard me out. I will forever be grateful for this.

Where would I be without my initial trustees? Bruce (RIP), Linda, Cheryl, and Cathy. Thank you for providing me with a deep and wide foundation of what school board governance is all about. You took a chance on me that August night in 2009, and I hope I have made you proud.

Dean, Anna, Greg, Dee, Cherie, and J.P.---I consider us principled, persistent, and purposeful. In our time together, despite the societal, cultural, and financial shifts, Panama's "Excellence in Education" mission was never diminished or compromised. We understood governance. Our mission each 2nd and 4th Tuesday of the month was all about the children. While we may have held our differences, the respect between us is monumental and an example to school boards nationwide.

Linda, Paula, Bryan, and Tom—the new school of board members. I am now on my way out and place the tradition and torch of Panama Buena Vista into your hands. Remember KIDS first!!!!

Remember the rules of governance despite the outside forces. Stay together as a governing body and team, and remember you were elected to serve all the students in the district.

A word of thanks also to my excellent editor, Dr. Vanessa Stretch, Ph.D. for her patience and diligence.

And finally, to the employees, stakeholders, community, parents, and students at Panama Buena Vista Union School District. I'm sure there were votes you disagreed with but bless you for allowing me to serve you. I did my best, and all I can say is ...

Thank you for trusting me!

Keith Wolaridge

Bibliography

Chapter 1

Brickell, H. Paul R. (1988). Time for Curriculum: How School Board Members Should Think About Curriculum, What School Board Members Should Do About Curriculum

Burgett, J. (2013). The Art of School Boarding: What Every School Board Member Needs to Know (K-12 School Leaders Series) (p. 61). Education Communication Unlimited. Kindle Edition.

King, M. L. (1988). The Measure of a Man. United Kingdom: Fortress Press.

Kingkade, T. (2022). Liberal parents are joining the school culture wars – but conservatives are way ahead https://www.nbcnews.com/politics/politics- news/democrats-republicans-school-board-elections- parents-rcna52698.

Lugg, C. and Gallagher, J. (2007). Effective School Board Leadership: A Synthesis of the Literature (2007)

Nierenberg, A. (2021). The Conservative School Board Strategy https://www.nytimes.com/2021/10/27/us/the- conservative-school-board-strategy.html? Auth=login google1tap&login=google1tap

Sinek, S. (2009). Start with why: great leaders inspire everyone to take action. Penguin Books.

Sinek, Simon. The Infinite Game (p. 106). Penguin Publishing Group, Kindle Edition

Ballotpedia. (2022). Analysis of school district and board member characteristics 2022. https://ballotpedia.org/Analysis_of_school_district_and_b

oard_member_characteristics,_2022

Chapter 2

Campbell, D., & Fullan, M. (2019). The Governance Core. School Boards, Superintendents, and Schools Working Together. George, B. (2015). Discover Your True North. Wiley Publishing.

Holzman, M. (2017). "Why school board races should remain nonpartisan." Washington Post

Iowa Association of School Boards (2001). "The Lighthouse Inquiry: School Board/Superintendent Team Behaviors in School Districts with Extreme Differences in Student Achievement," A Paper Presented at the American Educational Research Association, April 10-14, 2001. p.25.

Odom, K. (2014). "10 Questions Every School Board Member Should Ask". p.31 (Kindle Edition)

Maloney, R. (2023). "Oath of Office". American School Board Journal. p.31.

Maxwell, J. (2023). The 16 Undeniable Laws of Communication. Maxwell Publishing. p.93.

McDonald, R. & Contant, D. and Marshall, A. (2020). A Nonpartisan Model for Developing Public-Service Leaders. https://store.hbr.org/product/a-nonpartisan- model-for-developing-public-service-leaders/H05JH7.

National Association of State Boards of Education (2023). "The Role of School Board Members in Education Governance" (2023).

National School Boards Association. (2000). "The Legal and Ethical Responsibilities of School Board Members: An Overview". Texas Association of School Boards. "A Guide to Ethical Decision-Making for School Board Members" https://www.tasb.org/services/board-development-services/resources/for-new-board-members/code-of-ethics.aspx

White, R. Rachel S. White and Mark Y. Lineburg (2023). https://kappanonline.org/school-boards-superintendents- work-concert-white-lineburg/

Chapter 3

Beadie, D. (2005). Five Habits of High-Impact School Boards Bryant, J. (2016). Success is a lousy teacher. It seduces smart people into thinking they can't lose. https://selfmadesuccess.com/success-is-a-lousy-teacher-it- seduces-smart-people/Crawford, C. (2015). Breadcrumbs to Making it Great. Volume 2. p 193.

Education Law Association. (2020). "The Legal and Ethical Responsibilities of School Board Members".

Guilliam, J. (2020). Seats At The Table. School Board Members Perspectives on Race & Racism. Mexican American School Boards Association. (p. 211).

Panza, M. (2023). The True ABCs of School Board Service. American School Board Journal.

Chapter 4

Allen, J. (1902). As A Man Thinketh.

Branson, R. (2011). "Richard Branson on When Inexperience Is An Advantage," Entrepreneur Magazine.

Goleman, D. (1995). Emotional Intelligence

Great Schools Staff (2021): Six ways to boost your teen's emotional intelligence https://greatschools.org/gk/articles/tips-to-boost-teens-emotional-intelligence/

Holiday, R (2018), Holiday 25 Ways To Kill The Toxic Ego That Will Ruin Your Life. https://medium.com/thrive-global/25-ways- to-kill-the-toxic-ego-that-will-ruin-your-life-32a0bd2c0932

Kennedy, J. F. (1956). A Profile in Courage.

Kiviland, C. (2018). "Successfully Managing Emotions and Behavior." Healthcare Executive 33 (1): 68.

Lencioni, P. (2016). The Ideal Team Player: How to Recognize and Cultivate the Three Essential Virtues

Sharon, R. (2023) The Unseen Powerhouse of Emotional Intelligence in Leadership (LinkedIn) https://www.linkedin.com/pulse/unseen-powerhouse- emotional-intelligence-leadership-ron-Sharon/

Singua, Mehula. (2016). Personal Blog. "Your Ego is Not You Amigo" https://lifeinprogress290296.wordpress.com/2016/09/03/your- ego-is-not-your-amigo/

Walton, D. (2012). "Emotional Intelligence: A Practical Guide,

Chapter 5

Corasaniti N. (2016). You Won the Election. Now What?", The New York Times.

Hersh, E. (2020). "The Problem Isn't the 'Mobs.' It's the American Political Imagination,"

Reiff, N. (2016). "Winning the Election is Only Half the Battle: A Guide to Governing," Forbes.

Sill, Kaitlyn (2020). The Conversation
Steir, Max. Harvard Business Review. "A Nonpartisan Model for Developing Public-Service Leaders"

Epilogue

Anderson, C. (2017). White Rage: The Unspoken Truth of Racial Divide Martin Luther King, Jr., The Measure of a Man; United Kingdom, Fortress Press. (171)

Black in America (2018). Martin Luther King Jr. "Letter from Birmingham Jail (143).
Comer Contrell, C. www.quoteland.com/topic/Inspirational-Quotes/234/

Du Bois, W. E. B., (1903). The Souls of Black Folk. New York, Avenel, NJ: Gramercy Books.

Edwards, J. (2018). Black in America. "Stranger in the Village" p. 115. Broadview Press.

Glaude E. (2021).YouTube. "Take Giant Steps to Full Self" Glaude, E. (2016). Democracy in Black. How Race Still Enslaves the American Soul

Kaufmann, L. (August 2020). 6 Baldwin Quotes about race. https://www.pbs.org/wnet/americanmasters/6-james-baldwin-quotes-race/15142/

Kramer, P. and Atkins, K. (February 2023). "What is Black Fatigue and Code Switching and Why Do they Matter to Organizations? National Institute of Health. https://www.edi.nih.gov/blog/opinion/what-black-fatigue-and-   code-switching-and-why-do-they-matter-organizations
McCluney, C. Robotham, K. Lee. S. Smith R, Durkee M. (2019). The Costs of Code Switching. Behavior is necessary for advancement but takes a great psychological toll. Harvard Business Journal. https://hbr.org/2019/11/the-costs-of- codeswitching
We hope you enjoyed Keith Wolaridge. To order copies of this book or to schedule a speaking engagement, please write:

Email: keithw@fivepillars.biz Website: www.keithwolaridge.com

Facebook:

Conversations with Cousin Keith
https://www.facebook.com/authorspeakerprofessor/?modal=ad
min_todo_tour

LinkedIn:

https://www.linkedin.com/in/keith-c-wolaridge-262473a/ Twitter:
@kwolaridge

Instagram:

@authorkeithc

YouTube:

Conversations With Cousin Keith

Book Title

Now available on Amazon!

Made in the USA
Columbia, SC
04 December 2024

47278265R00072